ACROSS THE CENTURIES

Teaching Units for Timeless Children's Literature from a Christian Perspective

Level E
Volume 1

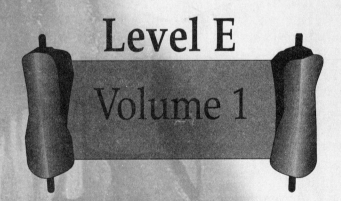

Author: Wendi Pollard

The Bronze Bow ❦ *Anne Frank: The Diary of a Young Girl*
Treasure Island ❦ *Anne of Green Gables*

Across the Centuries: Level E: Volume 1

Managing Editor	Sharon R. Berry, Ph.D.
Project Editor	Barry M. Morris, Ph.D.
Author	Wendi Pollard
Illustrator	Barbara Crowe
Production	Sherry Berry
	Donna Harden
	Sandy Kilgo

Printed and Distributed by
Convention Press
Nashville, TN 37234

Created and Developed by
Christian Academic Publications and Services, Inc.

All Rights Reserved
Copyright © 1998 Convention Press

Across the Centuries: Level E: Volume 1
ISBN: 0-7673-9172-1

CONTENTS

Preface 4

The Bronze Bow
      Introduction 5
      Instructional Plan 9
      Enrichment 31
      Masters 33

Anne Frank: The Diary of a Young Girl
      Introduction 49
      Instructional Plan 52
      Enrichment 76
      Masters 77

Treasure Island
      Introduction 95
      Instructional Plan 97
      Enrichment 123
      Masters 124

Anne of Green Gables
      Introduction 139
      Instructional Plan 142
      Enrichment 173
      Masters 175

Welcome to *Across the Centuries*, a series of teaching units for timeless children's literature from a Christian perspective. The volume you are using is one of many available for students in various grade levels.

> Level A — Preschool and Kindergarten
> Level B — First and Second Grades
> Level C — Third and Fourth Grades
> Level D — Fifth and Sixth Grades
> Level E — Seventh and Eighth Grades
> Level F — High School

In this series, books of exceptional literary quality serve as the basis for instructional units developed by gifted classroom teachers focusing on creative, proven techniques to engage and challenge students. Additionally, natural opportunities were taken to integrate each book with Biblical principles and a Christian worldview that incorporates character building aimed toward high ethical values.

The series provides unique resources for teachers and parents who want to convey a Christian perspective of life to their children and teens. Each volume contains four to five instructional units that present clear directions for teaching a unit from the introduction to instructional strategies to questions and answers to evaluation and conclusion. Masters designed for duplication present student exercises, vocabulary studies, background information, research projects, craft ideas and assessment instruments. In addition, masters provide the teacher with instructional materials and patterns. All masters are designed with art and graphic components to make them visually appealing to students. Answer keys appear in the text in conjunction with the teaching strategies. Each unit contains suggestions for enrichment including class activities, research methods, projects, field trips, crafts and summary experiences.

All materials are highly flexible and teachers are encouraged to select those activities which best suit the interests of their students and the time they have available. A unit can easily be implemented as a class project, as an optional, enrichment activity or as a challenge to only one or two students. The time devoted to instruction can thus vary from a full class period over several weeks to minimal interaction as students independently develop portfolios. Teachers can use all or part of a unit as they design and implement their instructional programs based on their knowledge of their classes. The materials are especially useful to parents in homeschooling or as enrichment to their regular school programs.

To achieve optimal success in teaching the units in this volume, begin by selecting a book that complements your curriculum. Read the entire unit and review all the masters and suggested activities. Based on the level and interests of your students and the time to be devoted to the material, plan your instructional program. Choose the activities, strategies and projects that best complement your goals. Prepare materials and copy masters in advance. Contact special guests and initiate any related projects through parent volunteers. Implement your plan and enjoy the results.

May you be blessed as you teach these selections of award-winning literature in relation to the wonderful words and works of God.

THE BRONZE BOW

by Elizabeth George Speare

Written by a beloved young adult writer, Elizabeth George Speare, *The Bronze Bow* is a story of fear and courage, love and hate, responsibility and carelessness. As it has a religious setting, students are faced with moral issues that are not found in many contemporary books. *The Bronze Bow* brings to light many ideas and beliefs that are essential for Christian young people.

OBJECTIVES:

1 Students will use multiple strategies to ascertain the meaning of vocabulary words, including word walls, webs, context clues, root words, affixes and synonyms.

2 Students will describe motives of characters and predict future behaviors based on those motives.

3 Students will compare and contrast character personalities, the differences in the settings, and the development of multiple themes.

4 Students will identify the symbols which occur in Daniel's story and explain how they could be seen in the Bible as well as in the world today.

5 Students will build a web explaining the theme of love versus hate and show how it connects to events in the book and key events in history.

6 Students in discussion will explain how the love of Christ appears in the story and how they might apply this same love in their own lives.

7 Students will predict the conclusion of events in the story using an effective organizational plan for writing.

8 Students will participate in class discussions, debates and small group activities.

SUMMARY OF THE STORY:

Set during the time of Christ, *The Bronze Bow* follows the life of one boy, Daniel, who finds the love and forgiveness of Jesus in the midst of his search for revenge. Daniel struggles between the worlds of crime and respectability. His hatred for the Romans contrasts to his discovery of Jesus. Throughout the story, hope unfolds as Daniel grows to love and understand the kingdom of God which Jesus proclaimed.

ABOUT THE AUTHOR:

Written by award-winning author Elizabeth George Speare, *The Bronze Bow* is a 1962 Newbery Medal winner. The author has won numerous awards including the Newbery Medal twice, a Newbery Honor citation, the Scott O'Dell Award for Historical Fiction, the Christopher Award, and the Laura Ingalls Wilder Award for her lifelong contribution to children's literature. Trained as an English teacher, Speare is considered one of the best historical fiction writers for young adults. She died in 1994.

PREPARATION FOR READING:

1 Select students as explorers to search for materials from the media center to build a classroom library. Student librarians can organize the materials and assist other classmates to find needed resources.

2 Assign a small group of students to draw and label a large floor map of the ancient world. Three-dimensional models can be built and placed on the map. Locations to include might be Rome, Jerusalem, Capernaum, Athens, Nazareth and Bethlehem.

3 After researching types of transportation in the ancient world, the students can build models of ancient sailing ships, chariots, caravans and wagons. Add these models to the floor map.

4 Select a group of students to add models to the floor map of the agricultural products grown in the Mediterranean world.

5 Weapons of ancient Rome were much different from the countries she conquered. After finding pictures of Roman weaponry, assign volunteers to build life-size models of the weapons and design a display called "Ancient Rome's Might." Add pictures of Roman soldiers and the portraits of famous Roman generals.

6 In a contrasting display entitled "The Weapons of God," let students make a hanging mobile of the armor listed in Ephesians 6. Include pictures of famous Christian heroes and a short description of their lives. Ask students to compare and contrast Rome's might to the power of the Holy Spirit in producing real change.

7 Pre-teach some of the vocabulary words on **Master I.1**.

Chapters 1–5: oleander, apprentice, zealot, legion, galley, skirmish, mottled, mutton, manacle, sentry, quaver, lentils, oppressor, furtive, infidel, linnets, phylacteries, turban, foolhardy, cohort

Chapters 6–10: pungent, vengeance, waver, sickle, talisman, chasm, rivet, forge, reek, horde, reconcile, skinflint, derisive, anvil, treacherous, brooding, pallet, fetid

Chapters 11–15: gape, garrison, unfathomable, litter, tether, scythe, tunic, sullen, intricacy, shekel, prod, ferocity, niche, alabaster, skein, molten, peer

Chapters 16–20: contempt, tetrarch, legation, scruples, lustrous, scrutiny, consignment, phalanx, cutthroats, swarthy, swagger, flogged, cavalry, plume

Chapters 21–24: confer, pious, atone, jostle, jest, homespun, garland, reprisal, infinite, dismal, coax, crevice, concoction, mezuzah, luminous

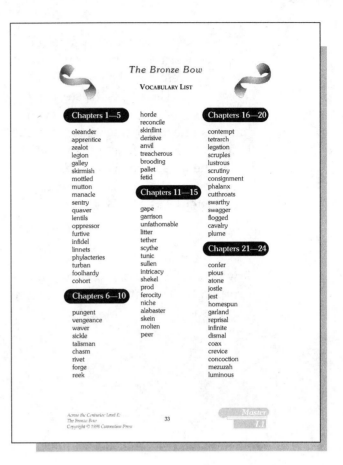

8 Some suggested vocabulary activities are:

1) Build a Category Word Wall. As students read the text, let them list vocabulary words they discover in one of two categories: Ancient Words/Modern Words.

2) Using the Category Word Wall, assign several vocabulary words to individual students. Each word should be researched. Using index cards, the students can illustrate the word and write it in a sentence. Add these cards to the Word Wall.

3) Have students select nouns and verbs from the vocabulary words. Use the list to play "Charades."

4) Build a vocabulary book in the shape of the land of Galilee. Students can add words at the opening of each chapter.

5) Introduce a "Word of the Day" to the class. The word is added to a poster of "Power Words" to replace "tired words in our daily writing."

6) Student teams can make up games and puzzles to teach the vocabulary words to peers.

9 Draw a large web on a poster. Keep the poster available throughout the study. The center of the web will be "Love versus Hate." As the story is read, have students connect key events that illustrate this theme to the center of the web. Add events in history that also fit this theme, such as World War II, Nero's persecution of Christians, etc. Use **Master I.2** as a worksheet for the class.

10 Refer to the Review Questions provided at the end of the unit. Plan to incorporate these into the discussions for each lesson.

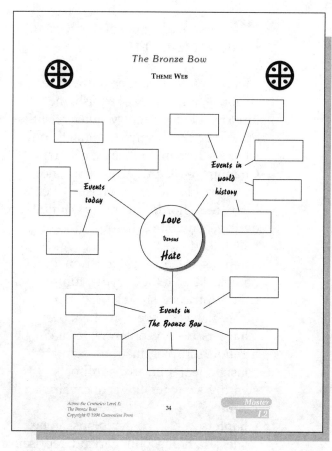

Instructional Plan

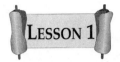 **Lesson 1**   **Chapters 1–2**

Daniel bar Jamin, an apprentice to an abusive blacksmith, has been hiding in the hills of Galilee for five years. He has joined a small band of criminals under the leadership of Rosh, who is planning a revolt against the Romans. He finds Joel bar Hezron and his twin sister, Malthace, wandering through the hills. Joel wants to join Rosh's band. He helps Daniel to rob a caravan and steal a slave. Joel meets Rosh and is recruited. Rosh orders Daniel to free the black slave, Samson.

1 Read Chapters 1 and 2. Discuss the setting. Use **Master 1.1** to provide background information about Judea and Galilee in 30 A.D. The master can be used as an overhead transparency. Have students complete the information as you present it in lecture format. Students could be assigned different portions of the lecture to present to the class.

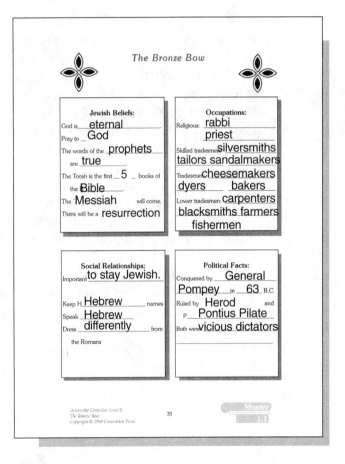

a) Political atmosphere — The Jews were slaves to the Romans. The Roman Empire conquered the known world. General Pompey conquered Galilee in 63 B.C. Herod, a Jewish king, betrayed his own people and worked for the Romans. Pontius Pilate, a vicious dictator, ruled as the Roman governor.

b) There were five classes of occupations. The religious class included the rabbis and the priests. The skilled tradesmen were merchants, silversmiths, tailors and sandalmakers. Tradesmen included bakers, cheesemakers and dyers. The lower tradesmen included carpenters, blacksmiths, farmers and fishermen. The lowest class was the slaves.

c) The social life of Galilee was summed up in one sentence: Important to stay Jewish. The people kept their Hebrew names. They spoke Hebrew. They dressed differently from the Romans.

d) There were important beliefs key to the Jewish faith. God is eternal. One should pray to God. The words of the prophets are true. The Torah is the first five books of the Bible. The Messiah will come. There will be a resurrection.

Across the Centuries: Level E:
The Bronze Bow

2 Use **Master 1.2** to focus on Daniel and Joel's different perspectives on life and Roman control. These boys are two of the main characters. How are they different? How are they the same? As students read the first several chapters, consider how the boys react to the same situations. The theme of love vs. hatred appears in these first two chapters. Give examples of both and have the students try to predict how these emotions may shape the characters and the story line.

3 Have the students draw a picture of Daniel's hillside home overlooking the village with the Sea of Galilee in the distance. What type of architecture exists in the village, and what colors seem to dominate the scene? Provide books on Biblical archaeology to assist the students.

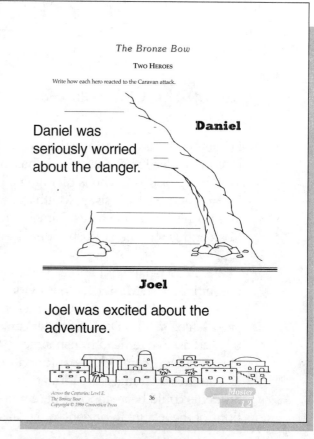

4 Obtain a chisel or file and piece of steel chain and have the students try to file through the steel. Re-read the passage in Chapter 2 where Daniel is filing Samson's chains. How much patience did this take for both Daniel and Samson?

5 Have the students prepare a newscast where they have an "exclusive" interview with Rosh and his followers. Interview them as to why they live the way they do, why they feel that they must steal from the townspeople and passing caravans in order to live, what is their ultimate purpose in living as criminals, and what do they see as their eventual contribution to the Israelite people? Videotape this interview.

LESSON 2 — CHAPTERS 3–4

After Daniel frees Samson, the former slaver becomes Daniel's protector. Simon, a fellow blacksmith, visits Daniel and talks him into returning home. Daniel's grandmother and his sister Leah are in desperate need. Leah is terrified of everything. In bed that night, Daniel longs for the hillside and wonders why he has come back. Daniel hears Jesus preach. He wants to follow Him until Jesus talks about repentance. Daniel's hatred of the Romans stops him from believing Jesus' message.

1 Read Chapters 3 and 4. Daniel faces many emotions in these chapters as he comes face to face with the reality he left behind. How does seeing where Daniel came from help us understand who he is? How is it hard for him to go back?

2 Compare Matthew 4:12–17 and Luke 4:31–32 with the passage of Jesus preaching in the synagogue. How does the author's description add to the description of these two Bible passages? How can the students relate more to these passages after viewing them through the eyes of the book's narrative?

3 Choose three inspirational speakers and find audiotapes or videotapes of their speeches. Have the students complete **Master 2.1** about why these speakers have been considered inspirational and then compare them with Jesus. As Jesus is the most dynamic speaker and teacher of all time, what characteristics did He have that would draw such crowds? Speakers could include Martin Luther King, Jr., Winston Churchill, Billy Graham, John F. Kennedy, Dwight L. Moody, Ronald Reagan, Franklin D. Roosevelt and local pastors.

4 The outlaws had a limited supply of fruits and vegetables, and any meat they had was stolen from neighboring farms. With the few vegetables they have available (cabbage, cucumbers and onions), direct students to write recipes that they could have made. Encourage them to be creative because they don't want to tire of having the same dish over and over again.

5 With the coming of Jesus, many people expected Him to fulfill different roles. He means different things to different people. To David, the Lord was his Shepherd (Psalm 23) because a shepherd is what the young David could relate to. Following the example on **Master 2.2**, have the students write what Jesus is to them.

6 Using **Master 2.3**, lead students to begin an analysis of the book's main characters. Students should include a one-sentence personality description and also list the character's strengths and weaknesses. This chart should be updated as the story and characterization develop.

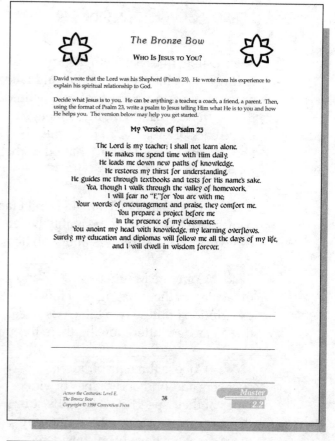

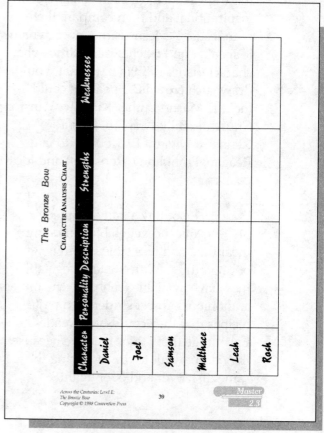

Lesson 3 — Chapters 5–6

After returning to the mountain caves, Daniel asks Rosh if he can go to Capernaum to find Joel. During his search, Daniel hears Jesus preaching. This time, Daniel angrily turns away because he sees Roman soldiers listening to the carpenter. Daniel meets Joel's father. Hezron, Joel's father, asks Daniel to leave his house because the boy is a Zealot and wants to revolt against Rome. Daniel is wounded and almost arrested by Roman soldiers. Thacia hides him and cares for him.

1 Read Chapters 5 and 6. Point out to the students how they have left Daniel's world and are now in Joel's world, but Jesus has been in both of them. Daniel's hatred is still extremely strong, and he acts on his feelings twice—once by not staying to hear Jesus because of the Roman soldiers, and another time by throwing a bowl at a Roman soldier. This hatred is strongly contrasted with the love that is shown by Jesus and Joel's family. Add these events to the web poster contrasting "Love versus Hate."

2 Discuss how fishermen earned a living in Bible times. Bring pictures or videos of re-enactments. Share with the students the methods these fishermen used, and then let the students brainstorm problems that they might have faced. Compare and contrast with how fishing is accomplished today.

3 Daniel could have been convicted of disobedience and disrespect, maybe even treason, because of his actions toward the soldiers. Research the laws during this period concerning disobedience to government authorities. What would have happened to him? What about today? Do the same laws apply? This would be the same time period that John the Baptist was arrested and executed. What laws had John broken? Did he receive a fair trial?

4 Daniel's problem with the Romans is that he resents being a slave. Many of the Jews just accepted their captivity and continued in their daily routines. The world today is captive to many things. Brainstorm with the students about how people are captive today. What are some situations in the world that really do make captives of people? Bring newspapers and have students find stories, ads and headlines that illustrate how the world is held captive. Have pairs of students build collages from the materials they collect.

5 Using writing journals, ask the class to react to one of the following questions: Did Daniel know that he was alienating Joel and his father? Did he do it on purpose? Why did he feel regret when he was asked to leave? If you were Daniel, how would you have handled the situation differently? Require complete paragraphs with a topic sentence and at least three supporting sentences and a summation sentence.

LESSON 4   CHAPTERS 7–8

As Daniel heals, Joel and Thacia read Scriptures and discuss the changes they would like to see politically. Daniel tells the story of his parents' deaths and the effect it had on his sister. Joel and Thacia decide to join Daniel in his oath of vengeance and agree to use the sign of the bow as their symbol. Daniel makes it back to the mountain safely. Rosh sends him to search for Simon. Daniel and Joel find Simon and Jesus together. Daniel sees Jesus' miracles and hears Him speak.

1 Read and discuss Chapters 7 and 8. These two chapters show a crucial period in Daniel's life. He is committed to a vow of death, yet he is drawn to Jesus' words of repentance and love. Focus on the story that Daniel tells about his parents and how these events have shaped his life. Help the students realize that Daniel chose the life of hate. He let his parents' death affect him this way, while Leah chose to hide from the pain. In direct contrast with this story in Chapter 7, you will see the healing power of Jesus in Chapter 8. How does this healing foreshadow what could happen to Daniel and his "illness." Who is the only one able to heal Daniel?

2 Ask students to retell the story of Daniel's parents and sister either orally to another person or by writing the story in their journals.

3 Discuss why the group chose a bronze bow as a sign of their commitment. *(lasts forever, unbreakable, never changing, hard, cold, a sign of war or power, way to kill an enemy, etc.)* Assign volunteers to make a model of a bronze bow. Have them be creative in the materials that they use and the extra touches that they add. Make sure poster board, string, markers, glitter, glue and other art supplies are available to the students. Add their bows to a bulletin board with reasons for their choice of this symbol. Leave room for a contrast to the effect of love in Lesson 12.

4 Have the students make a list of all of Jesus' miracles they can remember. Students can use Bible references to describe each miracle. After the activity is complete, use **Master 4.1** as a checklist of the miracles and where they can be found.

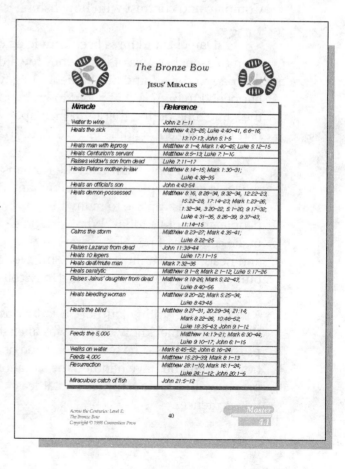

Across the Centuries: Level E: The Bronze Bow

5 Compare and contrast Daniel's story of his father's crucifixion with that of Jesus. What new details of his punishment does Daniel share in his story? How are the stories similar? How are they different? Assign students to research crucifixion, then discuss their findings in class. Why was this such a terrible way to die?

6 Assign the following questions as a writing assignment. Students may select one question. After discussing their answers with writing partners, students can assist one another in reconstructing and editing their paragraphs.

1) How does the vow that Daniel, Joel and Thacia make change Daniel's attitude toward revenge?

2) How do the people who are healed by Jesus feel? What kind of faith is required of these people before they can be healed?

3) How does the miracle of healing compare to the healing from our sin that Jesus gives? What kind of faith do we need to have?

4) How are we made whole spiritually, similarly to these people who had physical problems?

LESSON 5 CHAPTERS 9–10

Back on the mountain, Rosh has given Daniel his first robbery job to do alone. He completes the task but has compassion for the man at the last minute and gives him back his dagger. Rosh reprimands him. Soon Daniel discovers his grandmother is dying. He returns to his village to care for his sister and dying grandmother.

1 Read Chapters 9 and 10. Discuss with the students how Daniel is losing respect for Rosh and how his thoughts are turning toward Jesus. What is causing this division in his mind? How does he respond to it? Also, mention how Daniel is quick to respond to his family in need. What does this say about the change in his priorities? How does the evening with his grandmother and sister help him put his life into perspective? How does Daniel respond to being needed by his family?

2 In Biblical times, people did not have books or magazines. Instead, they had scrolls. Let the students choose a Bible verse and make a scroll on which to write it.

3 As Daniel's family spends time talking, he mentions how proud he has always been of his name. Many of the main characters' names have Biblical significance (Daniel, Joel, Leah, Simon). Let students research these names in the Bible and discuss the stories connected to each of them. Then have the students relate characteristics from the Bible stories with the characters in *The Bronze Bow*.

4 The robbery is a very significant point in Daniel's life as he realizes that he may not want to be a part of Rosh's band. Let students act out this scene, focusing on Daniel's response to the situation and how he reacts to Rosh's reprimand when he returns to the cave. Let the students express more than is written in the book; let them experience what Daniel may have been feeling.

LESSON 6 — CHAPTERS 11–12

After the grandmother's funeral, Daniel decides to watch over Leah. Simon offers Daniel the blacksmith's shop, making him promise not to cause trouble with the Romans. Leah learns to trust Daniel and her new surroundings, and she begins to take over the chores. Daniel is forced to wait upon a Roman soldier. He almost loses his temper when he catches the soldier watching Leah. Daniel recruits Nathan, a young boy, to work for Rosh. The secret group of young revolutionaries reaches over twenty members.

1 Read and discuss Chapters 11 and 12. Daniel begins a new life in these chapters, and it proves to be a difficult transition for him to make. However, he does succeed, and students can discuss his perseverance and changing characterization. Daniel's extreme hatred for the Romans is now focused on one young soldier. What would happen if Daniel had accepted this young man? What is the significance of the soldier gazing longingly into their home?

2 Breadmaking is a lost art. Divide the class into groups; assign each student in the group to bring one of the ingredients for making bread. Spend a day baking and sharing the bread.

3 Daniel and Leah are young adults who have suddenly found themselves alone in the world. Ask the students how they might budget their time and money so that they could survive in the world. Children in Bible times were taught survival skills at a younger age, but students today still need to understand how expensive it is to live comfortably.

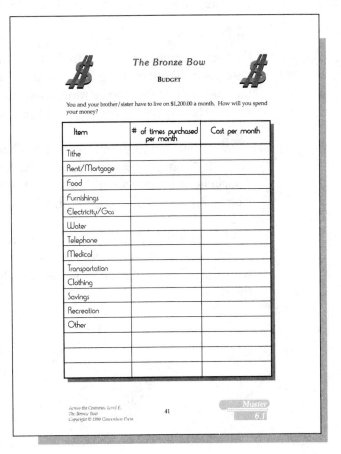

Given a budget of $1,200.00 each month (based on $7.00 per hour), how would the students spend it? What are necessities, and what are merely frivolous extras? Use **Master 6.1** for examples of items that need to be taken into consideration. Use the newspaper classified ads and the shopping guides to help students formulate a realistic budget. When students complain of insufficient funds, ask them to suggest potential solutions. As they conclude the need for a better paying job, help them think through the education and qualifications they will need.

4 Divide the class into teams of four. Have them discuss the questions and be prepared to offer their conclusions in a later classroom discussion. Use the following questions as team discussion topics: Did Daniel really have a choice in staying in the village with Leah? What were his other options if he did have a choice? Who supported him in his decision? Who opposed him? What does his decision say about his character?

LESSON 7 CHAPTERS 13–14

Leah continues to emerge from her shell. Joel and Thacia visit. Thacia becomes Leah's first friend. Daniel repeats to Leah his angry dedication to overthrow Rome. Daniel and Leah argue over meeting the Roman soldier. Daniel angrily leaves Leah and goes back to the mountain caves. Then he discovers he doesn't really fit with Rosh's group anymore. He returns to find that Leah has retreated into her shell.

1 Read and discuss Chapters 13 and 14. These two chapters primarily focus on Daniel's relationships with those around him. Joel is a true friend. They can disagree without causing hard feelings. When Thacia arrives with Joel, Daniel's feelings for her seem to be more than friendship. Daniel is breaking away from Rosh. He also recognizes a deep obligation to his sister.

2 Point out to the students that Thacia is a beautiful young lady, both inside and out. Using magazines, let volunteers design a collage of what they believe Thacia is like. They should describe her appearance, her family life, her personal traits, and her relationships with others.

3 Jewish weddings are different from the weddings that most students are familiar with today. Let volunteers research and report the traditions of a Jewish wedding. They can invite a Jewish family to share their wedding experience with the class.

4 When Daniel arrives back on the mountain, he realizes the differences that have grown between him and Rosh's band. Using the chart on **Master 7.1**, discuss with the class how Daniel has changed. Make sure that they use specific examples.

5 Distribute **Master 7.2**. As Leah re-enters the world of reality, she discovers the friendship of Thacia and a Roman soldier. Daniel's hatred of all Romans brings their points of view into conflict.

Note: The event showing Daniel and Leah's conflicting attitudes toward the Roman soldier could be included on the students' Love versus Hate web (Master I.2).

Ask the class to work in small groups to determine the reasons for Leah's attitude toward the Romans as compared to Daniel's point of view. Jesus has a special love for little children. Arrange to spend a class period with a preschool or kindergarten class reading to the children or playing with them. At the end have the students volunteer what they learned through the experience and what they would like to try if they had the opportunity again.

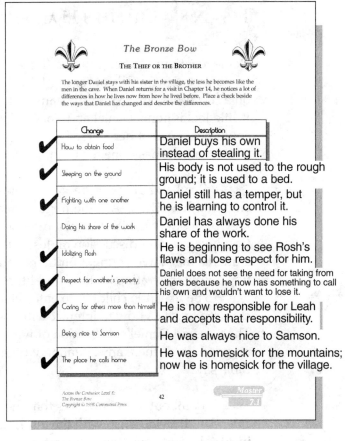

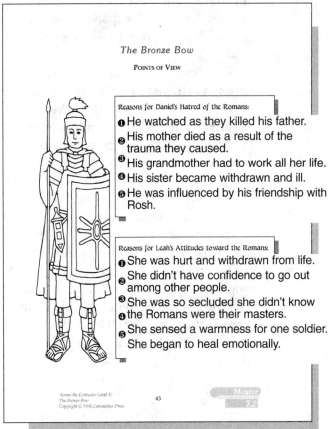

Across the Centuries: Level E:
The Bronze Bow

LESSON 8 CHAPTERS 15 AND 16

Daniel continues to be drawn to the teachings of Jesus. Leah listens eagerly as he recounts Jesus' miracle of raising Jairus' daughter from the dead. Rosh sends Joel on a secret mission to find the names of the rich Jews who will honor a Roman. While Joel is gone, Daniel and Thacia discuss Jesus' love. They wonder if He could heal Leah of her fears. Daniel gives Thacia the little bronze bow as a thank-you for all she has done for Leah.

1. Read and discuss Chapters 15 and 16. First, ask students to read and discuss Matthew 17:20. Ask them if they really believe in the power of prayer. Do they pray out of habit? Do they pray because it is the "right" thing to do? Conduct a second discussion on Jesus' love for children. As middle-schoolers, the students may have younger brothers and sisters or they have experience babysitting. How frustrating do they find little children? Why does Jesus say that we need to be like little children to enter His kingdom? How does Jesus' opinion of children teach us how to interact with them? A third discussion should focus on Thacia's and Daniel's discussion of lying. Thacia makes the comment that there is no good lie. Is there any situation where lying is appropriate? What does the Bible say?

2. Point out to the students that the Hebrew calendar is different from today's calendar. Provide them with the information about the Hebrew calendar as it was in 30 A.D. and have them illustrate it. Is it easier or harder than the one that exists today? Does it make sense?

3. Jesus and Rosh are the two characters portrayed as revolutionary leaders in this book. Using **Master 8.1** let the students work in pairs, groups or individually to complete the comparison and contrast of Jesus and Rosh.

4. Write these questions on the board. Ask students to write a short essay answer of the questions in their journals. What is starting to happen between Daniel and Thacia? What feelings are beginning to show, and what are the two doing about them? What may be holding Daniel back from saying anything?

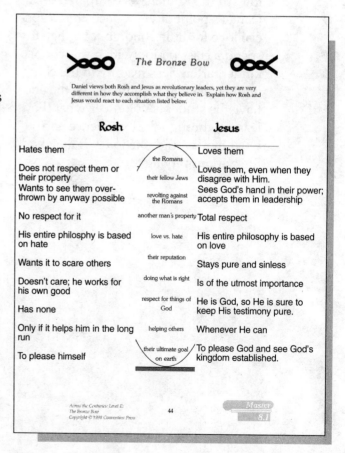

Lesson 9 — Chapters 17–18

Rosh has become more dangerous. Joel works harder and harder as a spy. Daniel begins to believe that Rosh is wrong. The villagers are threatening to stop Rosh's attacks. Thacia warns Daniel that Joel has been captured. Daniel rushes to ask Rosh's assistance. Rosh refuses. Daniel gathers his friends and devises a plan to save Joel.

1 Read Chapters 17 and 18. One of Daniel's most fundamental beliefs is challenged — that Rosh is the leader who will free his people from the Romans. Discuss with the students the concept of having a belief proven wrong. How difficult is that to accept? What has changed in Daniel's life as he fights to free Joel?

2 There is a great difference in Rosh's reputation and who he is in reality. Have the students complete **Master 9.1** in order to differentiate between this reputation and reality. Then discuss how reputations are often different from reality. Identify examples, and show how a false front can mislead people.

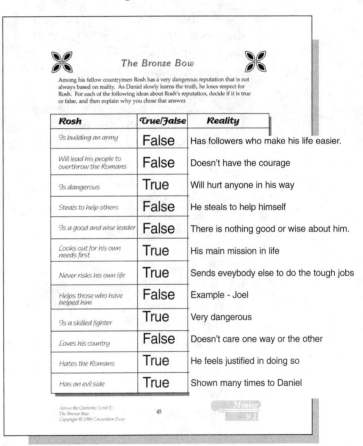

3 With Joel about to be sent to the galleys, it is important to know more about this common punishment in Biblical times. What was involved in being sentenced to the galleys? How many people survived the galleys? Let the students research the galleys and build models.

4 Have the class act out the passage of the argument between Daniel and Rosh with a special emphasis on Daniel's highly emotional state and Rosh's lack of any emotion.

5 Ask students to pretend they are Daniel and are facing the task of rescuing Joel from the guards. Have the students devise their own rescue plan.

6 Use the following questions for a writing assignment: Why do the townspeople choose Daniel to voice their complaints about Rosh? How does this make Daniel feel? Why do the townspeople make Daniel give Rosh the warning? Why don't they do it themselves? How does Daniel respond when Rosh doesn't listen to the warning? What would you have done?

LESSON 10 CHAPTERS 19–20

The boys are waiting to ambush the caravan that is taking Joel to the galleys. Samson has followed Daniel to help him. Joel is rescued but Samson is dragged away by the soldiers. Nathan has been killed. Daniel is now welcomed by Joel's father. Joel decides to travel to a school in a new city. Daniel discovers Thacia will have a marriage arranged by her family. Everyone is concerned because the enemies of Jesus are growing much stronger.

1 Read Chapters 19 and 20. Nathan's death forces Daniel to realize how difficult overcoming the Romans will be. Discuss with the students what it would be like to lose all freedom and then regain it. Was Joel's life different after being rescued?

2 In the process of rescuing Joel, two lives have to be sacrificed. Let students discuss the reasons people willingly make such sacrifices. What values are so important that students would risk their lives? Can students think of Biblical examples of similar sacrifices?

3 Arrange for the class to argue the pros and cons of arranged marriages. Divide the class into two debate teams. Allow 10 to 15 minutes for the teams to prepare their arguments. Organize the debate into the following seven sections:

Opening Statement	Questioning
First Argument	Debating / Arguing
Second Argument	Closing Statement
Third Argument	

4 Review the development of the story line, especially the building of tension toward a climactic outcome. Help students list the issues that must be resolved in the further development of the story. Have them predict the ending for "and they lived happily ever after." Because most real stories don't have ideal solutions, ask students what other endings are potential.

Answer key for Master 11.1

1. Daniel, Thacia, Marcus (soldier)
2. through the door of Daniel's shop
3. surprised but calm
   She is usually scared of everything.
4. He seemed homesick.
5. Marcus
6. over the garden wall
   When Daniel was not at home.
7. They both were a little bit sad and scared.
8. She learned to trust a stranger, and he gave her friendship.
9. He was a captive of Romans, not a true Roman.
10. fine, expensive fruit
11. She liked Marcus and knew there was nothing wrong in their friendship.
12. Answers will vary
13. a special friend who treated him like a friend instead of an enemy just because he was a Roman soldier
14. became very ill and shut inside herself
15. It almost destroyed it.
16. He was a Roman soldier and she was a Jew; her brother hated Romans.
17. Answers will vary.

Across the Centuries: Level E:
The Bronze Bow

LESSON 11   CHAPTERS 21–22

Daniel travels to Capernaum to warn Jesus of His enemies. As they talk, Jesus shows Daniel that his focus should not be on vengeance, but on love. Jesus asks him to give up his hate. Daniel goes to see Thacia and admits that he cares deeply for her. Later Leah admits she has accepted a gift from the young Roman soldier. Daniel threatens to kill the young soldier. Leah once again retreats into her own private world.

1 Read Chapters 21 and 22. The primary passage in these chapters is Daniel's conversation with Jesus. Have the students imagine what it would be like to have a conversation with Jesus. What would they talk about? What would it feel like to be able to talk to Jesus face to face? Discuss the conversation between Thacia and Daniel. Is it noble of Daniel not to want to bring Thacia into his life when he is still worrying about his vow? Is Thacia justified in her response?

2 What is the Day of Atonement? Have the students research what the holiday celebrates. Provide bulletin board paper to teams of four and allow them time to design their own murals about the Day of Atonement.

3 Compare and contrast the story of Nicodemus in John 3 with Daniel's nighttime visit with Jesus. What similarities can be made in what they talked about? What similarities can be made in the circumstances of how the visits took place? What differences can be noted?

4 Have the students analyze Leah's relationship with the young soldier. Using **Master 11.1**, the students will need to determine what actually was the relationship, then judge its meaning.

5 Use the following sentences as a story starter:

• If I could have one conversation with Jesus here on earth, it would be about . . .

• I would want to tell him . . .

• I would want Him to tell me . . .

Across the Centuries: Level E: The Bronze Bow

Lesson 12 — Chapters 23–24

In despair over Leah's illness, Daniel searches for Jesus and a miracle. He meets his old friend Simon who tells him that Jesus is the Messiah. Returning home, Daniel finds Leah sick with the fever. Thacia arrives, bringing Jesus with her. Jesus heals Leah. Daniel pledges his life to his new savior.

1 Read Chapters 23 and 24. Discuss with the class why Jesus was such a "controversial" person in His day and age. Why didn't Jesus fit what the Israelites expected in a Messiah? Was Daniel's reaction understandable? Place the following headings on the board to aid in the discussion:

WANTED!

A Political Savior from Roman Oppression	A Personal Savior and a Spiritual Kingdom

2 After Leah is healed and Daniel makes his decision to follow Jesus, the following question is asked: "Was it possible that only love could bend the bow of bronze?" Ask students to interpret this question. Why was the bronze bow originally chosen as the group's symbol? *(It was unbending, never to change from a commitment to hate and destroy the Romans.)* Why is the bow now bending? What is the power of love to change a life? Can love change lives today? How? Do students know examples of how love can change hearts? Add students' comparison to the bulletin board constructed in Lesson 4.

3 Compare the story of the Feeding of the Five Thousand with the Biblical account found in Matthew 14:13–21, Mark 6: 30–44, Luke 9: 10–17 and John 6:1–15. What would have been some other comments from people who witnessed this miracle?

4 If the class started the book with a newscast/interview with Rosh and his followers, use a newscast to close the book. Summarize all of the major events in the book with individual reports. Videotape the production to be shown to the class. Include Galilee's weather report, holidays coming up and commercials.

5 As a class, or individually, write a summary of what the next book could be concerning Daniel's life. Where does life take him now that he follows Jesus? What happens between Daniel and Thacia? What happens to Joel, Leah, Simon and Marcus? Let the students be as creative, yet as realistic, as possible.

6 Use the following question as a story starter: After you are saved, when is it the hardest to show God's love or to act like a Christian?

7 Provide a review and evaluation of the unit using any of the following options.

1) Refer to the Review Questions provided and select or modify questions that reflect your emphases in teaching the unit.

2) Evaluate written assignments and/or projects submitted by students.

3) Ask students to respond to the unit. What were their most/least favorite parts of the story? Characters? Activities? Why? What life lessons can be learned from the book?

4) Administer either a unit test you develop or the Unit Test provided on **Masters 12.1** and **12.2**.

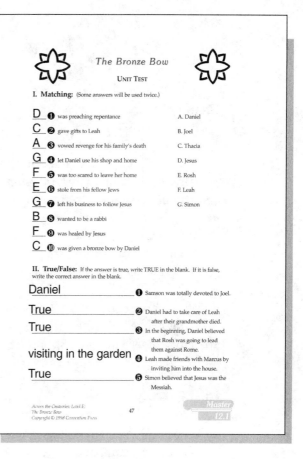

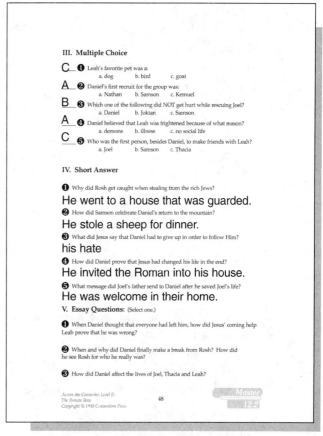

Review Questions

Chapters 1–2

1. How old is Daniel? *(18)*
2. How long has Daniel lived in the mountains? *(five years)*
3. Why has he run away? *(to escape a cruel apprenticeship)*
4. Why are Joel and Thacia in the mountains? *(They had always wanted to come and were getting ready to move.)*
5. What are some of the rumors about Rosh? *(that he will lead Israel against Rome)*
6. What is the only thing the men are to take from the slave caravan? *(a black slave)*
7. Why does Daniel offer to take care of the slave? *(to gain Rosh's attention and respect)*
8. What chore concerning Samson takes Daniel all night? *(filing off the chains)*
9. What is Daniel's opinion of Rosh? *(He's a good leader, afraid of nothing.)*
10. How does Samson respond to Daniel freeing him? *(falls at Daniel's feet; follows him around)*

Chapters 3–4

1. What is Daniel's main job in the cave? *(blacksmith)*
2. What is the controversy surrounding Samson? *(whether or not he can hear and speak)*
3. Why does Simon say it is safe for Daniel to come back to the village? *(Amalek is dead.)*
4. How does Leah act that makes Daniel sick at heart? *(frightened)*
5. What is it about his real home that makes Daniel homesick for the mountains? *(hunger, feeling stifled, his sister and grandmother's behavior)*
6. What is Leah's one skill? *(weaving)*
7. What is unusual about the man Simon wants to hear preach? *(Nazarene, a carpenter)*
8. How does Daniel respond to Jesus even before He starts speaking? *(He is drawn to him; his spirit leaps.)*
9. What bothers Daniel about Jesus' words? *(He spoke repentance instead of revenge.)*
10. Why is Daniel reprimanded for shouting at the Romans? *(He could cause harm to the village.)*

Chapters 5–6

1. What is the reason for Daniel's impatience on the mountain? *(not fighting the Romans now)*
2. Why does Rosh say that Joel won't want to help out once he is in Capernaum? *(He's got too much to lose.)*
3. Who makes Daniel leave when he comes to listen to Jesus? *(Roman soldiers)*

4. Why does Joel say that Thacia is acting differently now that they are in the city? *(She is putting on city airs.)*
5. Why does Joel's dad say that Zealots do not use good judgment when they go against the Romans? *(They don't think about how many Romans there really are.)*
6. Because of how Daniel acts at the meal, what does Hezron ask him to do? *(leave and not come back)*
7. What does Daniel do to the Roman soldier that gets him in trouble? *(throws a bowl of water at him)*
8. How does Daniel's shoulder get hurt as he runs away? *(He is hit by a spear.)*
9. Thacia tells Daniel that if he really cared for Joel, he would do what? *(leave him alone)*
10. When Thacia tells Daniel good night, what does it remind him of? *(his mother's voice)*

Chapters 7–8

1. What book is Joel reading that talks about fighting back? *(Enoch)*
2. Why does Thacia say that God would not choose Rosh to bring in His Kingdom? *(Rosh is an outlaw.)*
3. What does Daniel's uncle do that causes trouble with the Romans? *(does not have the money to pay his taxes and argues with the Romans)*
4. When does Leah's behavior change? *(after spending the night at her father's cross)*
5. Daniel, Joel and Thacia make a vow to what? *(God's victory)*
6. What is their secret symbol? *(bronze bow)*
7. What has Daniel never admitted to himself while on the mountain? *(he was lonely)*
8. When Daniel needs some new blacksmith tools, where does Rosh send him? *(Simon/Capernaum)*
9. Why does Jesus say that it is not important that they wash their hands before the meal? *(The meal was prepared with love; prepare your hearts, not your hands.)*
10. What allows the people to be healed by Jesus? *(their faith in Him)*

Chapters 9–10

1. What does Daniel give back to the old man because he has pity for him? *(one of his daggers)*
2. When Rosh questions him about this, Daniel asks him what? *(whom they were fighting against)*
3. What does Daniel have in him that Rosh says will not let him succeed? *(a soft streak)*
4. What message does Daniel receive from Simon? *(His grandmother is dying.)*
5. When Daniel gets to town, how many days has it been since the neighbors had seen the old lady or young girl? *(10 days)*
6. What does the doctor say has made the grandmother last as long as she has? *(She wanted to see Daniel.)*
7. When night comes, what does Daniel notice about his surroundings? *(There is no light or food.)*

8. What story does Daniel tell to his grandmother as she lay dying? *(Daniel and his friends Shadrach, Meshach, and Abednego)*
9. What has always been his grandmother's favorite Psalm? *(Psalm 23)*
10 To Daniel, what does Leah's holding his hand mean? *(She trusts him; the demons don't have complete control of her.)*

Chapters 11–12

1. What does Simon ask Daniel to do that sounds like a request, but Daniel knows Simon is really helping him? *(to take over his shop and home)*
2. How does Daniel feel when he realizes that he must stay with Leah? *(trapped)*
3. What is the one request Simon makes of Daniel so that no one in the town is hurt? *(to serve the Romans when they come into the shop)*
4. Why is it difficult for Daniel to move Leah to Simon's house? *(She won't go outside.)*
5. How do the townspeople help solve this problem? *(They make a covered litter for her.)*
6. What is the townspeople's opinion of Daniel as a worker? *(He is a good worker.)*
7 What does Leah insist upon so that she can watch Daniel work? *(the door to the shop be left open)*
8. Why does Leah start weaving again? *(customers requested her)*
9. When the Roman soldier takes off his helmet, what is Daniel surprised to notice? *(He is very young.)*
10. How does Leah respond to seeing the stranger? *(surprised, but not scared)*
11. Why has the young boy who comes into Daniel's shop been beaten up? *(His father became a tax collector.)*
12. Why does Daniel say that Joel has chosen well in choosing Kemuel? *(He has a fiery spirit.)*
13. Daniel says that the boys who join their group must be willing to serve without what? *(without reward)*
14. How many boys eventually are in the group? *(21)*
15. Why does Daniel change the group's meeting place? *(He thinks the Roman soldier is watching him.)*

Chapters 13–14

1. What does Leah do with the money that she makes from weaving? *(puts it in her headdress as a dowry)*
2. Why does Daniel want Joel to meet the new recruit from the Street of Weavers? *(He has some foolish ideas that Joel can talk him out of.)*
3. What does Joel say that Jesus has helped him with? *(understanding some of the Law)*
4. What is the first beautiful thing Leah has ever owned? *(Thacia's green girdle)*
5. What does the salesgirl give to Daniel because she charged him too much for the cloth? *(a needle)*
6. Whose wedding does Daniel attend? *(Nathan's)*
7. Why does Daniel say that he will never marry? *(He has to fulfill his vow.)*
8. What remark does Leah make about the young soldier that makes Daniel think she has talked to him? *(She says he is homesick.)*

9. How does Samson celebrate Daniel coming back to the mountain? *(brings a sheep for dinner)*
10. When Daniel comes home, how is Leah? *(lifeless and sick)*

Chapters 15–16

1. Why does Daniel enjoy going to hear Jesus, other than hearing Him speak? *(seeing Joel and Thacia)*
2. Why does Daniel think Jesus' story about the Jews and Samaritans is foolish? *(Jews and Samaritans would never get along.)*
3. Which of Jesus' miracles does Leah most like to hear? *(Jairus' daughter being raised from the dead)*
4. Who is Jairus'? *(ruler in the synagogue)*
5. What does Leah state about Jesus and children? *(Jesus would never let anyone hurt children.)*
6. What does Daniel make to remind himself of his vow? *(bronze bow)*
7. What does Rosh want Joel to find out for him? *(names of the Jews who will attend a feast for a Roman)*
8. What idea does Thacia have for Joel to accomplish this? *(sell fish to the servants)*
9. What idea does Thacia have for making it seem like Joel has left town? *(to switch places with him)*
10. Thacia knows that Jesus' opinion about lies would be what? *(He would never approve of them.)*
11. What do the Roman soldiers make Thacia and Joel do? *(carry their packs)*
12. What does Leah offer to Thacia that has made her proud? *(the meal)*
13. What does Joel give to Thacia as a thank-you for what she has done for Leah? *(bronze bow brooch)*
14. What changes that makes Daniel not want Thacia to have to carry a pack on the way home? *(He cares for her.)*

Chapters 17–18

1. What does Rosh do that gets him caught the night of the big feast? *(robs from a house that is guarded)*
2. To the group of boys, who is the real hero? *(Joel)*
3. How do the boys outwit Rome? *(take apart a catapult)*
4. What happens that causes the townspeople to issue a last threat to Rosh? *(He steals their sheep one time too many.)*
5. What news does Thacia bring to Daniel about Joel? *(He has been arrested.)*
6. Where is Joel going to be taken? *(galleys)*
7. Who joins Daniel to help free Joel? *(Joktan)*
8. Who does Daniel wish it would have been? *(Samson)*
9. Whom does the group of boys elect as their leader? *(Daniel)*
10. For whose glory do the boys promise to free Joel? *(God's victory)*

Chapters 19–20

1. What does Daniel not expect to happen when he goes to rescue Joel? *(He does not expect to make it back alive.)*

2. Instead of breaking up when attacked, what do the Romans do? *(charge)*
3. Who saves Daniel's plan by distracting the Romans? *(Samson)*
4. What happens when Daniel is thrown against the rock? *(breaks his shoulder bone)*
5. What happens to Samson? *(wounded and taken to the galleys)*
6. Which other member of the group do they lose? *(Nathan)*
7. Who comes to help Daniel at the blacksmith shop? *(Joktan)*
8. What message does Joel's father send to Daniel? *(Daniel is welcome in their home.)*
9. Why does Joel feel that he has to run away from home? *(He is being sent away to school.)*
10. What request does Thacia have of Daniel? *(to come see her dance at the Day of Atonement festivities)*
11. What news does Joel have for Daniel about Thacia? *(Their father is arranging her marriage.)*
12. Why does Daniel say he will never marry? *(He has to fulfill his vow.)*
13. What does Joel tell Daniel to do about Jesus? *(warn Him about his enemies)*

Chapters 21–22

1. When Daniel goes to warn Jesus what does Simon say? *(He already knows.)*
2. Why can't Jesus see anyone that night? *(He is too weary.)*
3. What does Daniel tell Jesus that he is troubled about? *(Everything has failed.)*
4. Jesus says that Daniel cannot repay Samson's love with what? *(vengeance)*
5. What does Jesus say that Daniel must give up in order to follow Him? *(hate)*
6. Why does Jesus say that Daniel is not far from the Kingdom of God? *(He says Daniel is working for God's victory.)*
7. What does Daniel notice about Thacia's dancing? *(She obviously enjoys it.)*
8. How does Daniel admit to Thacia that he likes her? *(He will never forget her face.)*
9. What is the special gift Leah receives? *(expensive fruit)*
10. How do Leah and Marcus become friends? *(talking over the garden wall)*
11. How does Daniel's anger affect Leah? *(Her new confidence wilts.)*

Chapters 23–24

1. What is Daniel's only hope in seeing Leah get better? *(Jesus healing her)*
2. What are the people calling Jesus that gives Daniel hope? *(Messiah)*
3. What does Simon admit about Jesus leading against Rome? *(He will never do it.)*
4. Simon says that everyone is forced to make a choice. What choice does he make? *(Jesus)*
5. What event seems to make Leah even sicker? *(Her goat dies.)*
6. Why does Marcus come to see Leah? *(He hears she is sick.)*
7. Why is it important that he see her soon? *(He is being transferred.)*
8. Who does Thacia bring with her to see Leah? *(Jesus)*
9. How does His coming affect the relationship between Daniel and Thacia? *(It makes Daniel realize that he wants a relationship with Thacia.)*
10. How does Daniel prove that Jesus has changed his life? *(He invites the Roman soldier into his house.)*

ENRICHMENT

1 Visit a blacksmith or silversmith in the local area.

2 Establish a pen-pal program with students in Israel (preferably Galilee). It can either be on an individual basis or as a class. Ask them about what Israel is like today, and what things are the same as two thousand years ago. Let them ask similar questions of America.

3 Watch a video of Israel as it was two thousand years ago so that the students can understand how and where Daniel lived. Compare the video to a film of modern Israel. How has the country changed? Would Daniel recognize his country today?

4 The idea of slavery is a major theme in the book. Let students research this topic. How does slavery in the book compare with what we think of as slavery today? How were slaves treated then? What slavery still exists today and how does it compare to slavery in the past? How were the slaves treated? What responsibilities did they have? How were they freed? What commands does Paul make to slaves in Titus 2? Students can write a two- to three-page paper on this topic.

5 Let students build a replica of a synagogue, Solomon's Temple in Jerusalem or a typical home of that time.

6 Take a field trip to a synagogue. Some synagogues will allow visits on a Friday night or Saturday morning so that the class can observe Jewish religious ceremony and interact with a teacher or priest.

7 Present some religious music of the Jews and discuss what is unique about it.

8 The social classes in Israel in 30 A.D. were very distinct and were usually divided on different lines from social classes in America today. Let students research what jobs were considered more important than others in Israel and who usually made more money. How does this compare with America?

9 Daniel is a fictional character based in a true historical setting. Let students brainstorm other stories within a similar setting. For example, the life story of the young boy who shared his lunch or what happened to Jairus' daughter. Challenge teams to develop a story board for a potential plot similar to the following:

- Darius is the innkeeper's son and falls in love with the new baby and his parents who have taken shelter in the barn.
- Darius grows up to become a cruel Roman soldier but suffers great turmoil of soul.
- When it looks like a mob will disrupt Jerusalem, he is called to duty in the city.
- At the last moment he must replace another soldier at the Crucifixion and is the one to confess, "Surely, this was the Son of God."
- He continues in faith but must sacrifice his career and finally his life for the cause of Christ.

The story boards can be shared and refined in class.

The Bronze Bow

Vocabulary List

Chapters 1–5

oleander
apprentice
zealot
legion
galley
skirmish
mottled
mutton
manacle
sentry
quaver
lentils
oppressor
furtive
infidel
linnets
phylacteries
turban
foolhardy
cohort

Chapters 6–10

pungent
vengeance
waver
sickle
talisman
chasm
rivet
forge
reek

horde
reconcile
skinflint
derisive
anvil
treacherous
brooding
pallet
fetid

Chapters 11–15

gape
garrison
unfathomable
litter
tether
scythe
tunic
sullen
intricacy
shekel
prod
ferocity
niche
alabaster
skein
molten
peer

Chapters 16–20

contempt
tetrarch
legation
scruples
lustrous
scrutiny
consignment
phalanx
cutthroats
swarthy
swagger
flogged
cavalry
plume

Chapters 21–24

confer
pious
atone
jostle
jest
homespun
garland
reprisal
infinite
dismal
coax
crevice
concoction
mezuzah
luminous

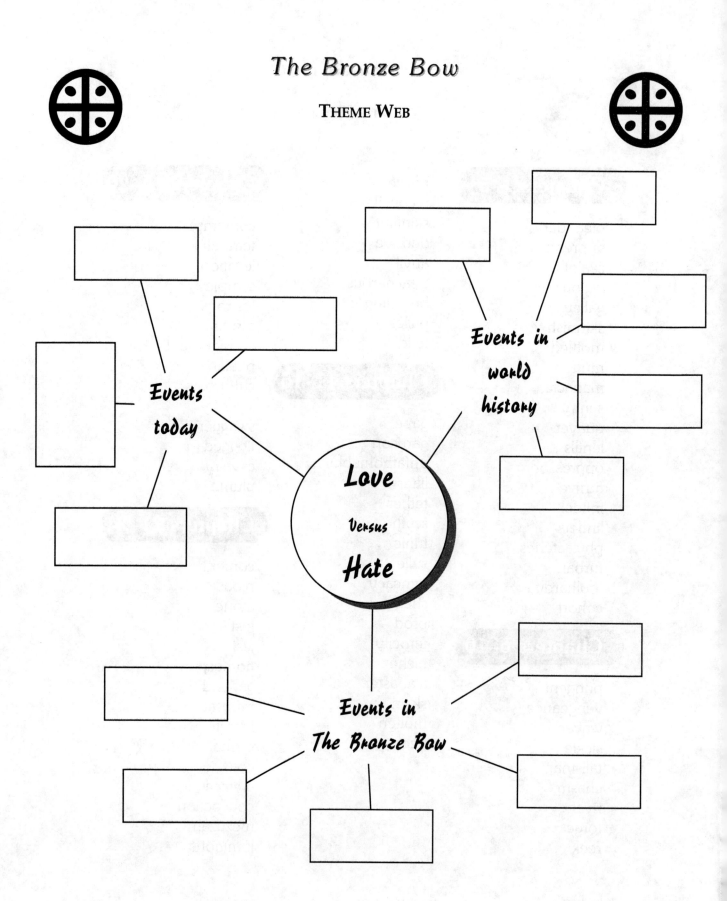

The Bronze Bow

Jewish Beliefs:

God is _____.

Pray to _____.

The words of the _____ are _____.

The Torah is the first _____ books of the B_____.

The M_____ will come.

There will be a r_____.

Occupations:

Religious: _____
_____

Skilled tradesmen: _____
_____ _____

Tradesmen: _____
_____ _____

Lower tradesmen: _____
_____ _____
_____

Social Relationships:

Important _____
_____

Keep H_____ names

Speak _____

Dress _____ from the Romans

Political Facts:

Conquered by _____
_____ in _____ B.C.

Ruled by H_____ and P_____

Both were _____
_____.

Across the Centuries: Level E:
The Bronze Bow
Copyright © 1998 Convention Press

The Bronze Bow

TWO HEROES

Write how each hero reacted to the Caravan attack.

Daniel

Joel

The Bronze Bow

As you listen to each speaker, answer the following questions.

Speaker's Note Card

❶ How well does he use body movements and hand gestures to make his or her point?

❷ Is his or her voice forceful and strong? Or is it quiet and sincere?

❸ Does the speaker use humor in order to make a point?

❹ What about eye contact? What does the speaker look at: the audience, floor or sky?

❺ What rating would you give the speech on a scale with 10 as excellent?

Speaker 1: _____

❶ _____
❷ _____
❸ _____
❹ _____
❺ _____

Speaker 2: _____

❶ _____
❷ _____
❸ _____
❹ _____
❺ _____

Speaker 3: _____

❶ _____
❷ _____
❸ _____
❹ _____
❺ _____

Best Speaker: _____

Explanation: _____

The Bronze Bow

Who Is Jesus to You?

David wrote that the Lord was his Shepherd (Psalm 23). He wrote from his experience to explain his spiritual relationship to God.

Decide what Jesus is to you. He can be anything: a teacher, a coach, a friend, a parent. Then, using the format of Psalm 23, write a psalm to Jesus telling Him what He is to you and how He helps you. The version below may help you get started.

My Version of Psalm 23

The Lord is my teacher; I shall not learn alone.
He makes me spend time with Him daily,
He leads me down new paths of knowledge,
He restores my thirst for understanding.
He guides me through textbooks and tests for His name's sake.
Yea, though I walk through the valley of homework,
I will fear no "F," for You are with me;
Your words of encouragement and praise, they comfort me.
You prepare a project before me
In the presence of my classmates.
You anoint my head with knowledge, my learning overflows.
Surely, my education and diplomas will follow me all the days of my life,
and I will dwell in wisdom forever.

_____

_____

_____

_____

_____

_____

_____

Across the Centuries: Level E:
The Bronze Bow
Copyright © 1998 Convention Press

The Bronze Bow

Character Analysis Chart

Character	Personality Description	Strengths	Weaknesses
Daniel			
Joel			
Samson			
Malthace			
Leah			
Rosh			

Across the Centuries: Level E:
The Bronze Bow
Copyright © 1998 Convention Press

The Bronze Bow

Jesus' Miracles

Miracle	Reference
Water to wine	John 2:1–11
Heals the sick	Matthew 4:23–25; Luke 4:40–41, 6:6–16, 13:10-13; John 5:1-5
Heals man with leprosy	Matthew 8:1–4; Mark 1:40–45; Luke 5:12–15
Heals Centurion's servant	Matthew 8:5–13; Luke 7:1–10
Raises widow's son from dead	Luke 7:11–17
Heals Peter's mother-in-law	Matthew 8:14–15; Mark 1:30–31; Luke 4:38–39
Heals an official's son	John 4:43-54
Heals demon-possessed	Matthew 8:16, 8:28–34, 9:32–34, 12:22–23, 15:22–28, 17:14–23; Mark 1:23–26, 1:32–34, 3:20–22, 5:1–20, 9:17–32; Luke 4:31–35, 8:26–39, 9:37–43, 11:14–15
Calms the storm	Matthew 8:23–27; Mark 4:35–41; Luke 8:22–25
Raises Lazarus from dead	John 11:38–44
Heals 10 lepers	Luke 17:11–19
Heals deaf/mute man	Mark 7:32–35
Heals paralytic	Matthew 9:1–8; Mark 2:1–12; Luke 5:17–26
Raises Jairus' daughter from dead	Matthew 9:18-26; Mark 5:22–43; Luke 8:40–56
Heals bleeding woman	Matthew 9:20–22; Mark 5:25–34; Luke 8:43-48
Heals the blind	Matthew 9:27–31, 20:29–34, 21:14; Mark 8:22–26, 10:46–52; Luke 18:35–43; John 9:1–12
Feeds the 5,000	Matthew 14:13–21; Mark 6:30–44; Luke 9:10–17; John 6:1–15
Walks on water	Mark 6:45–52; John 6:16–24
Feeds 4,000	Matthew 15:29–39; Mark 8:1–13
Resurrection	Matthew 28:1–10; Mark 16:1–24; Luke 24:1–12; John 20:1–9
Miraculous catch of fish	John 21:5–12

The Bronze Bow

Budget

You and your brother/sister have to live on $1,200.00 a month. How will you spend your money?

Item	# of times purchased per month	Cost per month
Tithe		
Rent/Mortgage		
Food		
Furnishings		
Electricity/Gas		
Water		
Telephone		
Medical		
Transportation		
Clothing		
Savings		
Recreation		
Other		

The Bronze Bow

THE THIEF OR THE BROTHER

The longer Daniel stays with his sister in the village, the less he becomes like the men in the cave. When Daniel returns for a visit in Chapter 14, he notices a lot of differences in how he lives now from how he lived before. Place a check beside the ways that Daniel has changed and describe the differences.

Change	Description
How to obtain food	
Sleeping on the ground	
Fighting with one another	
Doing his share of the work	
Idolizing Rosh	
Respect for another's property	
Caring for others more than himself	
Being nice to Samson	
The place he calls home	

The Bronze Bow

POINTS OF VIEW

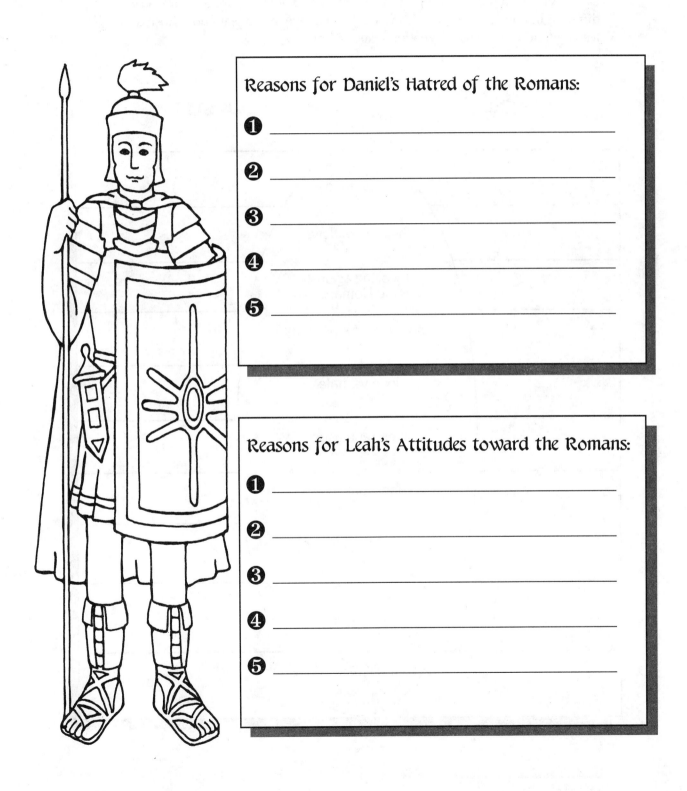

Reasons for Daniel's Hatred of the Romans:

❶ _____
❷ _____
❸ _____
❹ _____
❺ _____

Reasons for Leah's Attitudes toward the Romans:

❶ _____
❷ _____
❸ _____
❹ _____
❺ _____

Across the Centuries: Level E:
The Bronze Bow
Copyright © 1998 Convention Press

Master 7.2

 # The Bronze Bow

Daniel views both Rosh and Jesus as revolutionary leaders, yet they are very different in how they accomplish what they believe in. Explain how Rosh and Jesus would react to each situation listed below.

Rosh   Jesus

- the Romans
- their fellow Jews
- revolting against the Romans
- another man's property
- love vs. hate
- their reputation
- doing what is right
- respect for things of God
- helping others
- their ultimate goal on earth

Across the Centuries: Level E:
The Bronze Bow
Copyright © 1998 Convention Press

Master 8.1

The Bronze Bow

Among his fellow countrymen Rosh has a very dangerous reputation that is not always based on reality. As Daniel slowly learns the truth, he loses respect for Rosh. For each of the following ideas about Rosh's reputation, decide if it is true or false, and then explain why you chose that answer.

Rosh	True/False	Reality
Is building an army		
Will lead his people to overthrow the Romans		
Is dangerous		
Steals to help others		
Is a good and wise leader		
Looks out for his own needs first		
Never risks his own life		
Helps those who have helped him		
Is a skilled fighter		
Loves his country		
Hates the Romans		
Has an evil side		

Across the Centuries: Level E:
The Bronze Bow
Copyright © 1998 Convention Press

Master 9.1

The Bronze Bow

LEAH

Whether she knows it or not, Leah has learned to trust someone other than her brother and Thacia. How has her relationship with the young soldier helped her to become a stronger person? Analyze Leah's relationship with the soldier and determine how it has been beneficial to both of them.

1. Whom does Leah trust?

2. When was the first time Leah and the soldier saw each other?

3. How did she respond the first time? Why was this unusual?

4. What was it about the young soldier that made Leah want to talk to him?

5. What is the soldier's name?

6. How did the soldier talk to Leah? When did he talk to her?

7. Why were the two drawn to each other as friends?

8. How did trusting the soldier help Leah's self-confidence?

9. What information about himself had the soldier revealed to Leah that should have made Daniel like him more?

10. What gift did the soldier give to Leah to show his friendship for her?

11. Why was she so distressed about Daniel's reaction?

12. Were they just friends, or was there something more between Leah and Marcus?

13. How did Marcus feel about Leah?

14. How did Leah respond after Daniel forbade her to talk to Marcus again?

15. How do you think this affected Leah's emotional health?

16. What hindrances exist to prevent Leah and Marcus from becoming more than friends?

17. How might the author handle these conflicts as the story concludes?

The Bronze Bow

Unit Test

I. Matching: (Some answers will be used twice.)

____ ❶ was preaching repentance   A. Daniel

____ ❷ gave gifts to Leah   B. Joel

____ ❸ vowed revenge for his family's death   C. Thacia

____ ❹ let Daniel use his shop and home   D. Jesus

____ ❺ was too scared to leave her home   E. Rosh

____ ❻ stole from his fellow Jews   F. Leah

____ ❼ left his business to follow Jesus   G. Simon

____ ❽ wanted to be a rabbi

____ ❾ was healed by Jesus

____ ❿ was given a bronze bow by Daniel

II. True/False: If the answer is true, write TRUE in the blank. If it is false, write the correct answer in the blank.

_____ ❶ Samson was totally devoted to Joel.

_____ ❷ Daniel had to take care of Leah after their grandmother died.

_____ ❸ In the beginning, Daniel believed that Rosh was going to lead them against Rome.

_____ ❹ Leah made friends with Marcus by inviting him into the house.

_____ ❺ Simon believed that Jesus was the Messiah.

Across the Centuries: Level E:
The Bronze Bow
Copyright © 1998 Convention Press

47

Master 12.1

III. Multiple Choice

____ ❶ Leah's favorite pet was a:
     a. dog   b. bird   c. goat

____ ❷ Daniel's first recruit for the group was:
     a. Nathan   b. Samson   c. Kemuel

____ ❸ Which one of the following did NOT get hurt while rescuing Joel?
     a. Daniel   b. Joktan   c. Samson

____ ❹ Daniel believed that Leah was frightened because of what reason?
     a. demons   b. illness   c. no social life

____ ❺ Who was the first person, besides Daniel, to make friends with Leah?
     a. Joel   b. Samson   c. Thacia

IV. Short Answer

❶ Why did Rosh get caught when stealing from the rich Jews?

❷ How did Samson celebrate Daniel's return to the mountain?

❸ What did Jesus say that Daniel had to give up in order to follow Him?

❹ How did Daniel prove that Jesus had changed his life in the end?

❺ What message did Joel's father send to Daniel after he saved Joel's life?

V. Essay Questions: (Select one.)

❶ When Daniel thought that everyone had left him, how did Jesus' coming help Leah prove that he was wrong?

❷ When and why did Daniel finally make a break from Rosh? How did he see Rosh for who he really was?

❸ How did Daniel affect the lives of Joel, Thacia and Leah?

ANNE FRANK: THE DIARY OF A YOUNG GIRL

by Anne Frank

INTRODUCTION

A reflection of the thoughts and feelings of a young girl's heart, *Anne Frank: The Diary of a Young Girl* is especially relevant for young people today. The passage of time does not erase the confusion surrounding a teenager's journey to adulthood. Every student will be able to relate in some way to Anne's life as it is described in her diary. Given the historical setting of World War II and the suffering of Anne's family, this book will provide important lessons concerning thankfulness, forgiveness, love, patience and self-control.

OBJECTIVES:

1 Students will develop knowledge of the historical events surrounding Anne Frank's life and how those events are still affecting the world today.

2 Students will relate to Anne Frank as adolescents and apply the lessons that she learned to their own lives.

3 Students will demonstrate their knowledge of the importance of faith, family and personal beliefs in Anne Frank's life by showing how they are relevant in their lives today.

4 Students will demonstrate their ability to research a given topic to find specific information.

5 Using a variety of reference materials including the Internet, students will research and use information in the development of formal paragraphs and essays.

6 Students will analyze personality strengths and weaknesses of the main characters.

7 Students will establish topics, use a formal writing pattern including a beginning, middle, conclusion and transitions, will defend their topics with supporting details, and will edit their materials for grammar, punctuation and syntax.

8 Students will communicate their ideas through art, graphics, written work, debates and oral discussion.

SUMMARY OF THE STORY:

Anne Frank: The Diary of a Young Girl is the story of a young Jewish girl who goes into hiding with her family and friends in order to escape Hitler's persecution of the Jews in Amsterdam. Her story takes place over the two years that her family was in hiding. In her private diary, Anne Frank shares her dreams, her heartaches and the feelings of first love. Anne is forced to begin her teen years in hiding, yet many of her thoughts and ideas are as perceptive as any adult's. Her diary contains an important message which no one should ever forget.

ABOUT THE AUTHOR:

All that is known about Anne Frank is what was written in her diary. Born in 1929, Anne Frank would not survive her childhood to reach her dream of being a journalist. Yet her memory will live forever because of a diary she wrote during the most troubled two years of her life. Originally written in Dutch, *Anne Frank: The Diary of a Young Girl* has been translated into numerous languages and has sold millions of copies worldwide. The Broadway play, based on the book, has been awarded the Pulitzer Prize, the New York Drama Critic's Circle Award and the Antoinette Perry Award.

TEACHER NOTE:

Being the personal, private diary of a young girl, the book makes brief reference to topics not usually addressed in literature for this age group. These include Anne's monthly cycles, toileting, etc. One incident in which Anne thinks of kissing her friend shows her ambivalent feelings as she matures and develops an interest in Peter. You will need to decide how to handle these passages without giving them undue attention. Generally, it is best to answer any questions that arise but maintain the focus on the larger issues of the forced seclusion and how the group handles two years of isolation.

PREPARATION FOR READING:

1 Pre-teach some of the new vocabulary words students will encounter. Provide copies of **Master I.1** to be used throughout the unit. Select from the following vocabulary activities.

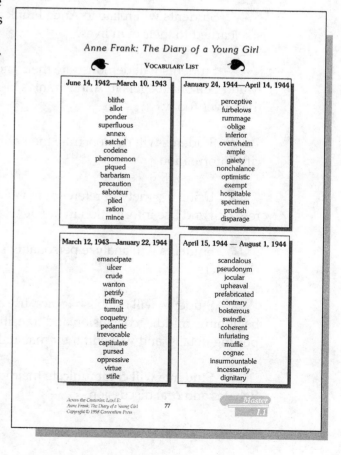

Across the Centuries: Level E:
Anne Frank: The Diary of a Young Girl

1) Provide copies of pictures that exemplify life in the 1930's to 1940's. Where applicable, write sentences using the vocabulary words as captions for the pictures.

2) Collect photocopies of World War II newspapers. List other words, with their definitions, that were in common use during that time period.

3) With the help of grandparents, make a list of the slang terms used by teenagers during the 1940's.

2 During World War II, it was a common practice to use a diary to describe the events of the day. Collect and exhibit a number of memoirs and diaries from this historical period. Encourage the students to skim the writings of famous generals, world leaders, soldiers and journalists. Since a number of these books are lengthy and quite difficult, ask the students to read only a few pages and report back to the group the information they discovered. Ask the students to explain how writing in a diary is different from fictional plots.

3 Invite an older adult who experienced World War II to share his/her memories or to read from a personal diary.

4 Invite students and other members of the community to bring family photo albums for an old-fashioned World War II day.

5 Students of Jewish, Japanese, German or Italian descent may find studies of World War II disconcerting. Emphasize the importance of discovering God's love and forgiveness, not man's inhumanity to man and the assignment of blame.

6 Invite older members of the community to share their memories of wartime rationing, the uncertainty of the news reports, the fears they had and the attitudes of the national government before, during and after the war.

7 Each student should obtain a diary to use during the study. This journal will be used for class assignments. After the unit is completed, encourage the students to continue recording their thoughts in a personal diary.

8 Collect some videotapes and audiotapes of key speeches from World War II leaders, such as Churchill, Hitler, Roosevelt, Stalin, Prince of Wales, King Edward, Mussolini and Chamberlain. Let students listen to these speeches and evaluate their messages.

INSTRUCTIONAL PLAN

LESSON 1 — JUNE 14 – JULY 5, 1942

Anne's diary begins a couple of days after her thirteenth birthday. Through these first entries, the reader finds Anne is interested in films, boys and her friends. She briefly discusses Hitler's anti-Jewish laws. Anne writes about Mr. and Mrs. Frank, Margot, Jopie, Lies, Peter Wessel and Harry Goldberg. She mentions her father's plan to "disappear" one day with no warning.

1 Distribute copies of the book and have students read the Afterward. Review the historical context of World War II and trace on a large map the movement of Anne's family from Frankfurt to Amsterdam.

2 Refer students to Anne's last entry (1 August, 1944) to skim or read aloud. Focus on the phrase "little bundle of contradictions" and let students discuss how this phrase might describe all students their age. Make a chart of the contradictions typical of their life experiences (one day acting very mature, another day childish; sometimes wanting parental direction, sometimes resenting it, etc.). Encourage them to add to the list throughout the unit and compare their experiences to Anne's as they read.

3 Remind students that this is a diary. There is no plot outside its historical context. It contains the descriptions of the events Anne experienced, along with her personal reflections. Throughout the book, students should identify this dual track of the reality of events and Anne's reactions to them.

4 Read the first section together. As the class starts this type of autobiography, focus on the historical and cultural events that Anne shares in her diary. Students should identify with many of Anne's struggles. Point out how a half-century does not completely change the ideas and emotions of a teenager. Characterization, irony, foreshadowing and the religious symbolism are important literary components to analyze with the class.

1) The eight central characters are portrayed in detail in this diary. In each student's diary, set aside several pages for character studies. Label the pages with the name of each major character. When reading the chapters, have the students add descriptions, especially the personality strengths and weaknesses of each character.

2) Define the term "irony" and provide several examples of ironic statements. Lead the class to write additional ironic statements. Set aside a section of the student notebooks to list the examples of irony encountered in the diary. The first irony, found on the third day, is that she doesn't plan to show this book to anyone. Discuss with the students what Anne would have written or done had she known this would be one of the most popular books of the 20th century.

3) Write this quote on the board: Mr. Frank said, "Make the most of your young carefree life while you can." Ask the students to explain the meaning of his words. Then write the word "foreshadowing" beside the quote. Have a student read the dictionary definition of the literary term. Point out that this quote is an example of foreshadowing. Assign a section of the diaries dedicated to listing examples of foreshadowing.

4) Throughout the unit there will be opportunities to compare Anne's suffering with Bible characters who also suffered for their faith. Ask the students to search for similarities between Anne's family and people in the Bible. Begin with the story of the Exodus.

5 Begin a large timeline on the wall. As the students document Anne's life before, during and after the Secret Annexe, show the events that were happening in the outside world, especially those related to World War II. Students will find this more relevant if they add American events to the timeline as well as European. Update the timeline every time a section is finished.

6 After discussing the true characteristics of friendship with the class, ask the students to write in their diaries a response to the following questions: Anne has been looking for a best friend, one that she can rely on and trust in completely. What are the characteristics of a true friend? What do you look for when choosing a friend? Are any of these characteristics the same as Biblical principles?

Lesson 2   July 8 – September 2, 1942

The next time Anne writes in her diary she has gone into hiding. Margot has received an S.S. notice ordering her to appear at the Nazi detention center. The family disappears into the Secret Annexe built by Mr. Frank. The Van Daans join the Franks in hiding. Anne explains what it feels like to disappear and to lose every freedom, even the right to go outside.

1 Students should read and discuss the second section. First impressions and various emotions are the two main focal points for this section. Anne makes immediate judgments of the Van Daans. By September 2 Anne has also described her own family members. What do the Franks feel when the call-up notice is given? What do they feel as they pack? What are the first few days in the Secret Annexe like? What feelings do they experience when the Van Daans come to live with them? How does it feel never to go outside and to have to be completely quiet? How would students react in similar circumstances? What activities could fill their days?

2 Use masking tape to mark off the size of the Secret Annexe. On a rotating basis place eight students into that area for the day. Ask them to plan how they would work together to organize the space. At the end of the day, discuss if the experience gave them any understanding of the claustrophobic living conditions the Franks had to endure. Then remind the students that the Franks and Van Daans lived here for more than two years.

3 Make available pictures of the World War II architecture in Amsterdam to show the class. **Master 2.1** should be displayed. Explain how the buildings were built so that the Secret Annexe was possible. Study the drawings provided by Anne on July 9, 1942, and discuss the assignment of space.

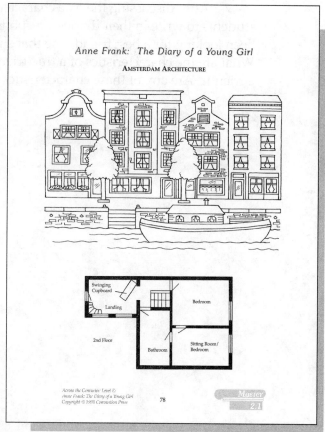

Across the Centuries: Level E:
Anne Frank: The Diary of a Young Girl

4 Ask the students to mentally pack their favorite belongings in order to disappear into hiding. Have the students think about where they could go if they had to disappear during a war. Discuss other groups in history who had to go into hiding, such as the Roman Christians into the catacombs. Ask the class to list the items they would bring with them. Anne and Margot were only allowed to fill one school satchel/backpack. Have each student bring to school a backpack filled with their most important items. Let them share what they have brought.

5 Let students choose an enrichment activity.

1) Anne and her father were forced to make blackout curtains using scrap pieces of material. Let the students try this project using the directions found on **Master 2.2**.

2) Nazi war propaganda offices forced newspapers to lie to the public. Divide the class into teams of reporters and editors. Ask the teams to construct and print a newspaper that tells the truth about what was happening to citizens who disagreed with the Nazi government during World War II.

3) The Internet has many World War II Web sites. Select sites appropriate for the classroom. Assign students research topics and Web sites. Information collected can then be organized in Hyperstudio presentations.

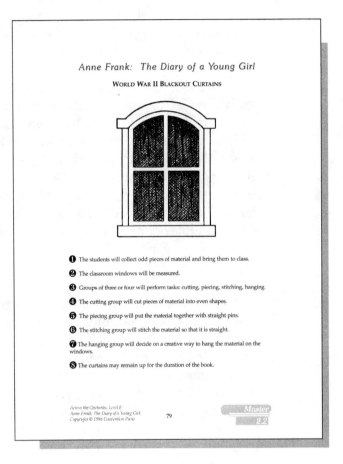

LESSON 3 SEPTEMBER 21 – OCTOBER 16, 1942

Anne records arguments between herself and almost everyone in the Secret Annexe. Of course, she perceives these quarrels as the fault of the adults because they do not understand her. Anne devotes one entry to the terrible stories of Jews suffering in the city.

1 Choose a trait that a small number of students share, such as eye or hair color or whether ear lobes are attached or hang down. Distribute six-pointed stars to this group and allow them to experience some acts of discrimination (no chairs, no talking, serving others, etc.). Let them relate their experiences to the unfair treatment of the Jews. Discuss again what their choices could and could not be.

2 Assign this section and discuss its general contents. Anne shows that she really is a 13-year-old girl as she deals with conflict. While they write their characterization notes, help the students differentiate between the ways that Anne deals with the different people in her home. Whom does she come into conflict with the most? Who has the least conflict? Was this justified or typical? Why does she not get along with certain people? Discuss Anne's comment, "You only really get to know people when you've had a jolly good row with them. Then and then only can you judge their true characters!" How true is this? Lastly, Anne encounters Peter a couple of times in this section. How do they relate to one another? Is there any foreshadowing of things to come? What is their relationship now? How does she treat him?

3 Have students dramatize the quarrels in this chapter. Encourage the class to write expanded dialogues for each quarrel.

4 On October 9 Anne makes the comment that "Germans and Jews are the greatest enemies in the world." Point out to the students there have been other conflicts throughout history. Divide the class into research teams. Assigning each group a different conflict, let them research the historical period and share their findings with the class. Each research team will be responsible for a portion of a bulletin board to design and maintain. Some examples of conflicting groups are England and America, Israel and Palestine, Roman Empire and Israel, Mongols and China.

5 Pose the following problem for discussion and then assign an essay to outline the answers in students' diaries: Anne is scared of being carried away to a concentration camp. Describe the feelings Anne experiences and how they would be similar to your own personal feelings about losing freedom forever.

6 Have artists in the classroom draw life-size pictures of Anne Frank and other family members. Then have student actors write a monologue that one of these characters might have spoken. Develop a class museum displaying the characters. Invite students to listen as the character speaks about his/her experiences.

7 In their diaries, have each student construct a Quotes Journal by dividing several pages into two columns. In the first column, students should write significant quotes found in the chapters. In the second column, they are to interpret the quote's meaning and relate it to their lives or to Biblical truths.

QUOTES JOURNAL

Chapter Title and Key Quotes	Applying the Quote to My Life

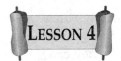

LESSON 4 OCTOBER 20 – NOVEMBER 19, 1942

Anne feels completely isolated from the rest of her family. She feels misunderstood and alone. The Secret Annexe members decide that they are able to accommodate one more refugee, Mr. Dussel. He will be sharing Anne's room.

1 Assign the reading and direct a general discussion of Section 4. Have the class analyze Anne's entry about her family. How does she express herself? What are some truths in her complaints? What might she be exaggerating? Do you ever have these same emotions? How many times is it just miscommunication? How could Anne have made her situation better? Start a new characterization page for Mr. Dussel. What does he seem to be like? How does his coming affect the rest of the Secret Annexe, particularly Anne?

2 Anne mentions one of Winston Churchill's most famous statements in her November 9 entry. Show a video of this statement or this part of the war. Have students discuss what Churchill meant by the statement and then decide how accurate he was.

3 When Mr. Dussel enters the Secret Annexe, Mr. Van Daan has written a brochure that explains the rules and procedures of the home. This brochure is a guide to what is allowed and not allowed in the Secret Annexe. Building on this idea, work with the class in designing brochures for the school, the grade level, the church youth group or your class. What points would they highlight? What is of importance for a newcomer to know? Are there any rules or guidelines? Decorate the walls and bulletin boards with the designs. As an extension of this exercise, the class could produce a video about the classroom. This would be used to introduce new students to the class or be given to the next year's class as an introduction to the new grade level.

4 Consider with the students Anne's comments on November 19 about being thankful for what the family has. Divide the class into groups of three or four. Ask the teams to list the names of people who have been in difficult situations but made the most of it. They can be from the past or present. How would they act if they were in any of these situations? Assign Scripture references to each group to apply to its discussion:

Philippians 4:10–13	2 Corinthians 4:6–9, 17–18
2 Timothy 4:16–18	2 Corinthians 12:9–10
Philippians 3:8–10	1 Peter 4:12–14, 19

Have students present their examples to the class.

5 Invite volunteers to build table-top dioramas of the Secret Annexe. Display the dioramas for younger classes. Assign students to explain why the Frank family was hiding from the authorities.

6 Write Mr. Frank's comment on the board: "If we can save someone, then everything else is of secondary importance." Have the class write in their diaries how this statement is true. How does it compare to Christian beliefs? They can add these reactions to the quotes journals.

7 Have the students add another section to their diaries, with pages divided into two columns. Write "Predictions" at the top of the first column and "What Actually Happened" at the top of the second column. Use this part of the diaries each time the story line moves toward a predictable event.

LESSON 5 — NOVEMBER 20, 1942 – MARCH 10, 1943

Anne knows now that Jews are disappearing everywhere. The horror of this new world is beginning to dawn on the family. Mr. Dussel and Anne are not making a good adjustment. Chanukah and St. Nicholas Day pass with a small gift for everyone. The threat of bombing raids makes the entire family anxious. The war is moving closer.

1 Assign the reading of Section 5 and lead a general discussion of the events. Refer to the chart related to "a little bundle of contradictions." Anne expresses many of these in this section to which students can relate. Update the timeline so that students can see the growing intensity of World War II.

2 Let students choose an enrichment activity and share their findings with the class.

1) Distribute copies of **Master 5.1a** and **b**. Students are to research the facts about the two holidays: Chanukah and St. Nicholas' Day. A fact sheet is provided below for **Master 5.1a** and **b**. Students can fill in the two webs on the master as they complete their research.

St. Nicholas Day

1. St. Nicholas is the Patron Saint of children and bakers.
2. The day is a reminder that Christmas day is coming soon.
3. December 6 is his feast day.
4. He is the original Santa Claus who brings good gifts for the good children and bad gifts if they have been bad.
5. Purpose of his day is to emphasize goodness, honesty, kindness, respect.
6. St. Nicholas was later transformed into the idea of Father Christmas or Santa Claus.

Chanukah

1. Called the Festival of Lights.
2. Lasts for eight days and is marked by the nine candles on the menorah.
3. The first candle, the shamash, lights the other eight candles.
4. Blessings are to be recited before kindling the candles each night.
5. All family members must be present when the menorah is lit.
6. The lights are lit either in the front window or by a doorway.
7. Celebrates the freedom won by the Maccabees for the Jews.
8. Focuses on unifying Jews around the world.

2) Use **Master 5.2** for a list of research topics about the life of Gandhi. Select students to search for information using CD-Roms, encyclopedias and the Internet. Each topic should be presented to the class. Students can write the key facts on the master.

3) Introduce the dreidel, an ancient toy that would have been very familiar to Anne and her family. Students can use **Master 5.3** to build dreidels. For best results, print the master on heavy paper.

4) There is an excellent Web site for holidays around the world: www.Holidays.net. Let students research and report various customs related to these holidays.

3) Organize an international day celebrating European holiday foods. Ask students to bring desserts, meats, vegetables and salads specific to the European countries involved in World War II. Encourage students to cook these dishes themselves and to bring a recipe to be added to an International Class Cookbook. Distribute this cookbook to each student in the class.

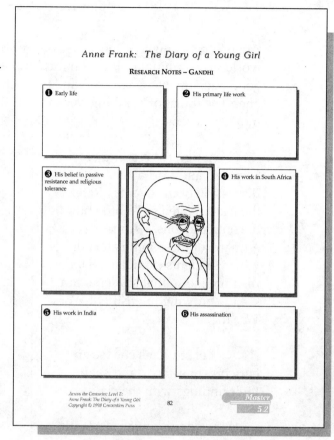

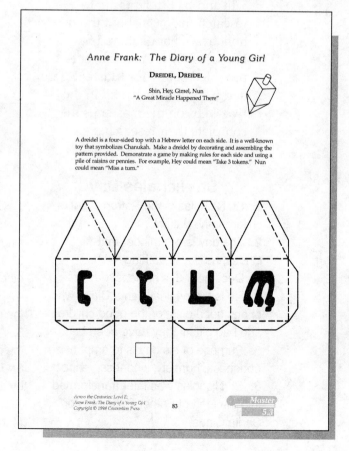

Lesson 6 — March 12 – June 13, 1943

The fighting is much closer to home. Air battles have caused food shortages. Ration cards and "black" money are more difficult to find for Jews who are in hiding. Thieves break into the building, but don't discover the family. Anne celebrates her 14th birthday and receives a poem from her father.

1 After students have read this section, discuss the sequence of events and Anne's reactions. Mr. Frank's birthday poem gives the reader a picture of Anne's character from another point of view. Discuss with the class the accuracy of Anne's viewpoint when compared to her father's. What positive things do we learn about Anne that she does not tell us?

2 Margot and Anne are allowed the opportunity of learning shorthand as one of their courses. Spend a week (about 10 minutes a day) teaching, or having someone teach, the class shorthand. Obtain a videotape with short lessons and introduce the students to this method of writing.

3 Ask the students to write a poem in honor of someone. They can mention positive characteristics and how others perceive him or her. Encourage them to use this poem as a tribute to someone they love and respect.

4 Anne closes this section with the following comment: "As the Benjamin of the family in hiding, I am really more honored than I deserve." Have the class review the story of Benjamin in the Bible *(Genesis 35 and 42)*. Add Anne's comment to the Quotes Journal and include its interpretation.

5 Finding food was a serious daily problem for Mr. and Mrs. Frank. As a mission project, involve the class in collecting food for a food bank, preparing meals for a homeless shelter or delivering food baskets to members of the community.

6 Frances Goodrich and Albert Hackett wrote the play, *The Diary of Anne Frank*, which was published by Random House. Work with the class to produce a dramatic version of Anne's story.

LESSON 7   JUNE 15 – AUGUST 3, 1943

The family has been in hiding for one year. Their radio is the only link to the outside world. More often thieves seem to be searching through the house. Heavy bombing raids and emergency sirens terrify everyone. There is good news when Mussolini resigns as dictator. The families begin to hope that they might survive the War.

1 Update the class timeline to include the war in Italy and in the Pacific. Discuss the Axis treaty between Germany, Japan and Italy and how that treaty would be weakened by Mussolini's resignation.

2 Assign the reading of Section 7 and follow it with general discussion of the text. Especially focus on how the War is affecting the residents of the Secret Annexe and how each reacts to stress. Ask why Anne thinks it is better to talk to herself than to others. Help students understand how conflicts resulted from sharing the cramped space and as a reaction to fear and stress.

3 Encourage students to act out the different scenarios on **Master 7.1**. Allow the class to decide the best way to solve each problem.

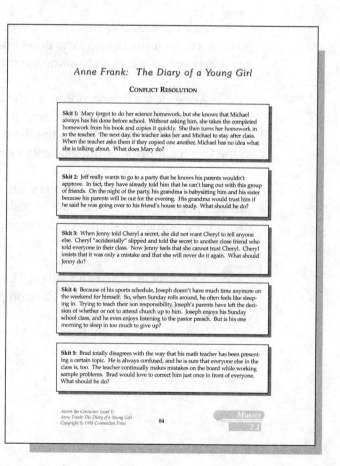

4 Using Mussolini's resignation, the bombing of North Amsterdam, or an air raid as the main story, lead the class in preparing a newscast for the events in this section. Divided into groups of 4-6 students, have each team write a 5-10 minute newscast that they will present to the class or have videotaped. They should focus primarily on the news, but they can also include other matters of interests such as food updates, weather, etc.

5 Use the following question for a diary entry: If you had been in hiding for a year, what would be your first wish when you were allowed to go outside again?

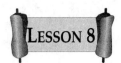

Lesson 8 August 4 – October 17, 1943

Anne gives a detailed account of their daily activities. The biggest news is Italy's unconditional surrender. Although this is wonderful news, the tension continues to build as the families in the Secret Annexe try to get along.

1 Review vocabulary and assign the reading of this section. Discuss the details of Anne and her family's life in hiding. Place a two-column chart on the board. Brainstorm with the class about these two categories and let students fill in the chart.

Impossible Situations in the Secret Annexe	Things I Take for Granted

2 Lead the students in writing a detailed description of their own typical day. Start with the alarm going off and write in half-hour increments up until bedtime. How might their days be different if they were in hiding? How could they handle the challenge of boredom?

3 Whatever the challenges of life in the Secret Annexe, life for Jews outside was much harsher. Direct students to research and complete **Master 8.1** "The Holocaust."

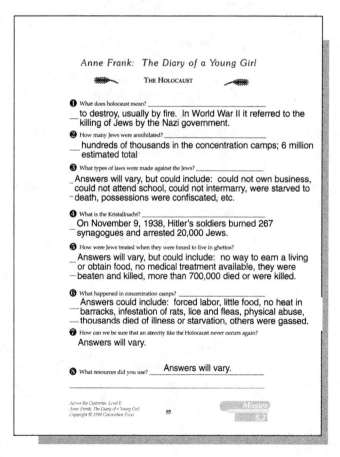

Across the Centuries: Level E:
Anne Frank: The Diary of a Young Girl

Lesson 9 — October 29, 1943 – January 5, 1944

Anne once again begins her entries with discussions of all of the quarrels that are occurring within the Secret Annexe. However, by the end of this section, she indicates that there is a peace in the Annexe. There is a new maturity in Anne's writing. Once again they celebrate Chanukah, St. Nicholas Day and Christmas. Anne has been dreaming of Lies and Granny. She feels she has deserted them.

1 Read and discuss the events in this section. Anne admits on November 8 that she thinks "after the war" will never really happen. What triggered this emotion? When she starts dreaming of Lies, she feels that she has failed in a friendship. Is this true? Or is it something that she could not help? Did she do something before she went into hiding that she now regrets? How is Anne maturing in her relationship with her mother?

2 Place a second chart next to the one describing Anne as a "little bundle of contradictions" and entitle it: Marks of Maturity. Throughout the remaining sections, as students identify changes in Anne that show maturity, list these on the chart. They could include:

- more patient
- understanding another's feelings or point of view
- less self-centered or self-focused
- ability to handle self and direct own activities
- more help and concern shown to others
- willing to give up a self-interest for the good of the group
- more responsible

Be sure students discuss items in relation to their own growing maturity.

3 The Passover Seder meal was another important holiday recognized by the Frank family. The Seder celebrated the Jews' release from Egyptian slavery. Invite a rabbi to explain the meal to the class. Have parents prepare the meal for the students. There is a full description of the meal on the Holidays Web site: www.holidays.net/passover/seder2.htm.

4 Ask the students to write a letter to Anne encouraging her not to give up. Then have the students select a person who has been suffering for an extended period of time. Invite them to write a letter of encouragement, a poem or to assemble a care package for a person in need.

LESSON 10 — JANUARY 6 – JANUARY 22, 1944

Anne has chosen Peter as a confidante. She adamantly denies that she is in love with him. Margot is treating her more like an adult now, so their relationship has improved. Anne finally admits that everyone is to blame for the arguments that occur from time to time.

1 While reading this section, ask the students to write a character analysis of Peter. Also assign them to list the activities in which everyone engages to fill the long hours in hiding. Discuss students' findings and the events of this section.

2 Discuss the following question with the class: If you could only choose one person to have as a friend while hiding, what type of person would you choose? Using **Master 10.1**, have the students identify the type of person that they would be most comfortable with when sharing their deepest thoughts and feelings. This could easily lead into a writing exercise: If you could only have one friend for the rest of your life, what kind of friend would it be?

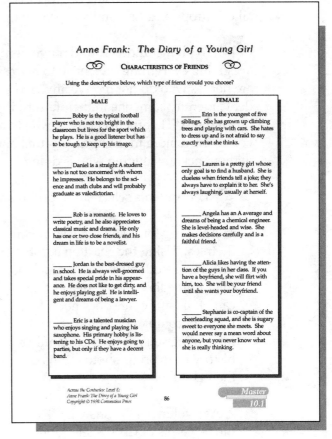

3 Share the following quote and begin a class discussion about relationships. Anne says, "I keep asking myself whether one would have trouble in the long run, whoever one shared a house with. Or did we strike it extra unlucky?" Let the students have an open discussion on this statement. They will have many opinions and probably a lot of personal experiences to share. Relate their discussions to Romans 12:18, 2 Corinthians 13:11 and 1 Thessalonians 5:13–18.

4 Working together in teams, direct the students to answer the following questions. Later the teams can present their opinions to the rest of the class. How will a close friendship between Anne and Peter change the relationships of the people in hiding? How will other family members react? Is it normal for Anne and Peter to enjoy being alone? Why would their parents want them to limit their time alone?

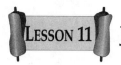

LESSON 11   JANUARY 24 – FEBRUARY 3, 1944

Anne and Peter are becoming better friends. Her mother has warned her to always be modest around boys. Anne has also become interested in family trees and movie stars. The most exciting event is the preparation for the invasion of Holland by England.

1 Assign the reading of Section 11 and discuss the events and Anne's reactions. What marks of maturity do students observe in Anne? (*Her feelings for Peter can be listed since these are a normal part of growing up.*)

2 Update the timeline of World War II events, showing Germany's control of all of Europe and England's approaching invasion.

3 With the underground movement, Anne makes a reference to Gentiles who are giving everything they have to help save the Jews. In her mind, these people are heroes who do not receive any credit. As an outreach project, have your students identify someone in their family, in the school, or in the community who is a "silent hero." Let them choose a way to honor this person and then carry it out. For an even more meaningful gesture, have your students honor these heroes without acknowledging who is doing it.

4 Let students select and report on an enrichment activity.

1) Anne has found an interest in family trees. Using the chart on **Master 11.1**, have students fill in as much of their immediate family tree as they can. If a family tree does not interest them, encourage them to share an interesting story from their family's history or to bring photographs of their childhood.

2) Ask volunteers to share book or film excerpts of Corrie Ten Boom's *The Hiding Place*. Compare and contrast the experiences the Ten Booms had with the life led by the Franks. They could also share parts of *Schindler's List* or other stories related to the Holocaust.

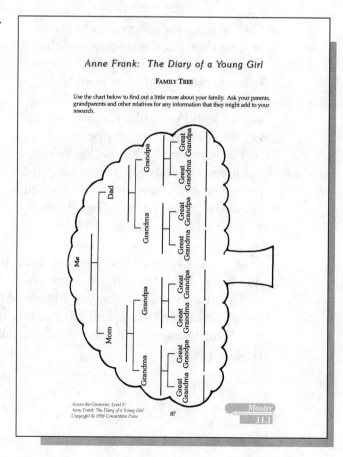

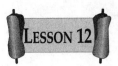

LESSON 12   FEBRUARY 12 – FEBRUARY 23, 1944

Anne is in love! Each entry in this section is devoted to the ups and downs caused by the first experiences of love. She struggles with whether or not Peter needs just a friend or some affection, too. Finally, she admits that as long as she has Peter with her in the Secret Annexe, she can be happy and content in hiding.

1 Read and discuss the events of Section 12. Since Anne is in their age group, students can relate to the feelings of a "crush" or a "first love." They know the uncertainty of what to say and how to act. Discuss with them how being in love changes Anne's perspectives.

2 Bring music from this time period, especially what people would have listened to in Europe. Anne makes a reference to the "Immortal Music of the German Masters." Who are these masters, and what is their type of music? Have the music playing in the background as you read or work on a project. Also provide sample music from the top American dance bands of the 1940's.

3 On February 23 Anne says, "The best remedy for those who are afraid, lonely, or unhappy is to go outside, somewhere where they can be quite alone with the heavens, nature, and God." Read the words to the hymn "How Great Thou Art," then direct students to search Psalms to support Anne's statement. What does God say about spending time alone with Him, worshiping Him in His creation, and turning to Him for refuge and comfort? Students should report their findings to the class or write an essay including the best verses they found.

4 Distribute copies of **Master 12.1** "Europe – 1944," and direct students to color the countries occupied by Germany. Add Allied army symbols and German army symbols to complete the map. Add symbols to show where the German concentration camps were established. Update the timeline as it relates to this section.

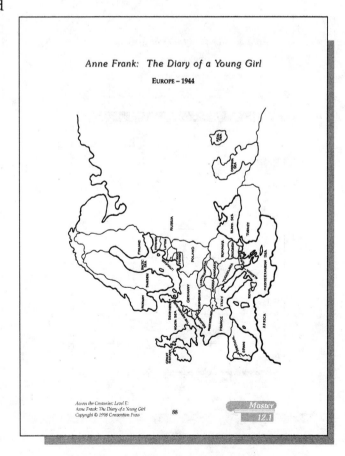

Across the Centuries: Level E:
Anne Frank: The Diary of a Young Girl

Copyright © 1998 Convention Press

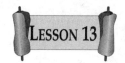

LESSON 13   FEBRUARY 27 – MARCH 15, 1944

There has been a robbery in the warehouse, and it appears to be an inside job. Anne is focused on her love for Peter. On March 7 Anne reflects on how she has changed over the past two years. She is honestly looking at herself, what her life is like now, and how it used to be.

1 Direct discussions after students read this section. Lead the class in analyzing the similarities and differences that Anne mentions about her and Peter. Are they accurate? Discuss the idea that the robbery was done by someone who had a key and worked in the warehouse. What would this mean to those in hiding? In the last entry, Anne gives a recitation of how each adult is responding to the constant tension of living in such close quarters. Are these comments accurate portrayals of each character's personality?

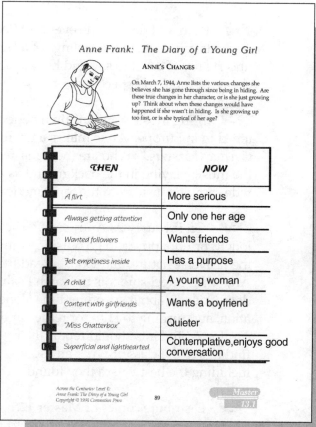

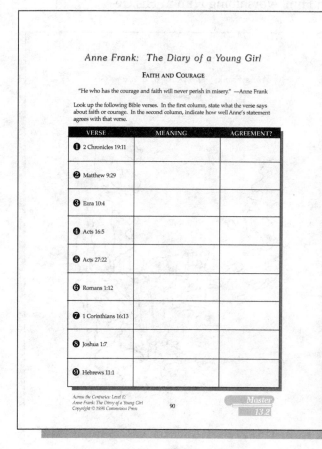

2 Using the information on March 7 and **Master 13.1**, analyze the changes which Anne has experienced over the past two years. Let the students try this first by themselves and then discuss it as a class.

3 At the end of the March 7 entry, Anne makes the following comment: "He who has the courage and faith will never perish in misery." Using the Bible verses on **Master 13.2**, have the students work in pairs to determine how Biblical this statement is. After reading and summarizing what each of the verses has to say, they can rate how Biblical Anne's statement is on a scale of 1–10.

Across the Centuries: Level E:
Anne Frank: The Diary of a Young Girl

4 Provide the following assignment for students to write in their diaries: On March 7 Anne states that she has a protective armor of "superficiality and gaiety" that she uses in order to protect herself from others. What is your protective armor, and how do you use it to protect yourself?

LESSON 14   MARCH 16 – MARCH 29, 1944)

Anne is growing more distant from her family. Anne comments that Peter keeps sane because he has his own room. Anne once again insists that she is much older than her fourteen years. Margot admits she is jealous that Anne has someone to talk with so openly.

1 After students read the section, lead a discussion of the events, including the following:

1) Anne's first complaint is that she does not have anywhere to call her own like Peter does. Discuss with the class the importance of having some place special to meditate on God's Word, pray or have a quiet time. Have the students place themselves in Anne's shoes. Why would it be even more important for her?

2) Update the political situation and add any major events that were occurring in the "outside" world to the timeline.

3) Discuss the irony of Anne's comment on March 29: "... it would seem quite funny ten years after the war if we Jews were to tell how we lived and what we ate and talked about here."

2 Jews around the world had been waiting for their return to Israel. Arrange for the class to see all or excerpts of *Exodus*, a classic movie that tells of the return of the Jews to Palestine and the rebirth of Israel.

3 For extra credit, let students research and report on assigned topics related to battles of World War II, one of the international leaders, occupied countries of Europe, the treatment of Jews, Zionism, the settlement of Palestine, the immigration of Jews to America, the recovery of artifacts and gold by survivors of the Holocaust, the capture and trial of war criminals, the treaties that ended the War, etc. Using CD-Rom reference materials, the Internet and other sources, they can develop Hyperstudio presentations to be shared in class.

LESSON 15   MARCH 31 – APRIL 14, 1944

Anne mentions that Stalin's Russia is an ally growing stronger every day. Hungary is now occupied by German troops. She shares her desire to become a journalist. There is another burglary. This time the police come to inspect the building. The police are on the verge of discovering the Secret Annexe, and this sends the occupants into a frenzy. The families have now realized how careless they have been at times.

1 Take time to update the timeline and to consider Russia's role in World War II. With the events that occurred between the Soviet Union and the United States after this war, would students have expected the Russians to fight with the Allies against Germany, Italy and Japan? What events were going on in Russia at this time that they would not want the Axis powers to take over the world?

2 Assign students to read and discuss Lesson 15.

1) Discuss the foreshadowing of Anne's statement, "I want to go on living even after my death!"

2) At the end of the April 14 letter, Anne makes this comment: "The unbosomings of an ugly duckling will be the title of all this nonsense." As a class, review the story of *The Ugly Duckling*. Then discuss how Anne is applying this story to her own life. Do most teenagers experience this same transformation?

3) Discuss with the class the comment Anne makes on April 4: "I can shake off everything if I write; my sorrows disappear, my courage is reborn." What activity do you find so refreshing that your worries seem to disappear when you do it? How could your quiet time with God help in the same way? You may want the students to respond to these questions in their diaries.

3 Refer to the chart listing "Marks of Maturity" and add students' observations. Discuss these two in particular.
• a desire and sense of future accomplishment
• an ability to reflect on one's self, to evaluate strengths and weaknesses and understand the changes that occur over time.

# LESSON 16 APRIL 15 – APRIL 28, 1944

The Secret Annexe occupants are almost discovered as Peter forgets to unbolt the door that he locks at night. Kraler is forced to break into his own building and try to explain to the other workers how it came to be locked. More security measures have been implemented since all of the burglaries, and this causes additional tension between the families. In her last entry, Anne discusses her conflicting emotions about Peter, their relationship, and where it is headed.

1 Assign the reading of Section 16 and discuss the events in general.

2 On April 17 Anne says, "I know almost for certain that Margot would never kiss a boy unless there had been some talk of an engagement or marriage." Discuss with the students how times have changed. What is acceptable for Christian couples? This is an excellent time to discuss what the Bible says about appropriate boy-girl relationships, regardless of what is acceptable by the world's standards.

3 On April 27 Anne lists everything that she learns in one day. Give the class the challenge of carrying around a pad of paper and a pencil for the day and document every time that they learn something new. It can be about any topic, and it can be the smallest detail. Then have them discuss their findings in class.

4 Discuss Anne's opinion of Peter: "Anne, be honest. You would not be able to marry him, but yet, it would be hard to let him go. Peter hasn't enough character yet, not enough will power, too little courage and strength. He is still a child in his heart of hearts, he is no older than I am; he is only searching for tranquillity and happiness." Is this an accurate assessment of Peter? Is it fair? Are maturity rates for boys and girls different? Is Peter likely to change in the future? Does Anne have a limited view of the future?

5 Explain that Princess Elizabeth is now Queen Elizabeth of England. Use the information on **Master 16.1** to assist with research and discussion.

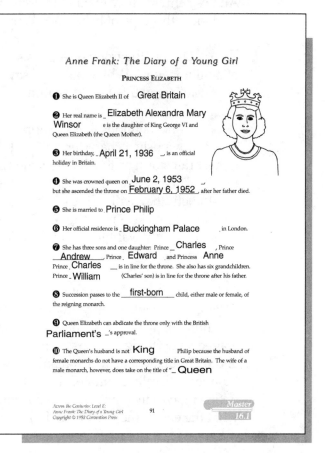

Across the Centuries: Level E:
Anne Frank: The Diary of a Young Girl

LESSON 17   MAY 2 – MAY 9, 1944

Peter and Anne tell Mr. Frank about their relationship. Mr. Frank asks Anne not to spend so much time with Peter. Anne feels that she is adult enough to make her own decisions. She writes her father a letter declaring her independence and accuses her parents of not supporting her enough. Mr. Frank is devastated. Anne realizes that she still has a lot of growing up to do.

1 Assign Lesson 17 and intersperse the reading with questions related to the possible motivations for each character's actions and the reactions that occur. Remind students that a mark of maturity is the ability to think ahead to the potential consequences of a particular choice. Sometimes this ability is clouded by our emotions and the immediacy of our desires.

2 Students will likely relate to the letter that Anne writes her father since most teenagers have felt these same sentiments. They never stop to think how their words and actions affect their parents. Use these entries to discuss why teens can feel this way toward their parents and why their reactions could hurt their parents. The Bible says, "Children, obey your parents in the Lord, for this is right. Honor your father and mother. . ." (Ephesians : 1–2a). How are actions similar to Anne's contradictory to what their behavior should be as Christians? How does God view this type of behavior? What should be done to make it right?

3 Discuss the irony of Anne's statement, "And these are the granddaughters of a millionaire." Why would she say this? Have the students list as many reasons as possible why this would be ironic.

4 Anne mentions that she appreciates Peter's honesty in their relationship. This is obviously a character trait that she desires in a future mate. Have the students brainstorm as to what they are looking for in a perfect mate. Let them make two lists. First, have them list the top ten attributes that come to their minds. Most likely, they will be rather shallow in nature. Then, have them review their choices and make a new top-ten list after stopping to think about what type of persons they really want to spend the rest of their lives with. Discuss with them the characteristics of greatest value.

5 On May 3 Anne states the following about the condition of mankind, "There's in people simply an urge to destroy, an urge to kill, to murder and rage, and until all mankind, without exception, undergoes a great change, wars will be waged, everything that has been built up, cultivated, and grown will be destroyed and disfigured, after which mankind will have to begin all over again." Is this thought Biblically accurate? Have the class search for verses in Romans 1–10 that define man's fallen nature, how a right relationship can be restored to God, and what the end of the world will bring. They can enter their reactions in their diaries.

Across the Centuries: Level E:
Anne Frank: The Diary of a Young Girl

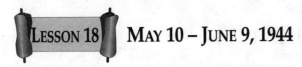

LESSON 18 — MAY 10 – JUNE 9, 1944

Anne has made a list of things that she would most like to know and is doing everything that she can to learn them. She reflects on how people are now blaming the Jews for the War. Jews, and those who are hiding them, are being arrested every day. The most important news occurs on June 6 — D-Day finally arrives. The end of the war is in sight, and they anxiously listen to all radio broadcasts about the event.

1 Assign and discuss the reading of this section. Let students suggest the potential changes D-Day and an Allied victory could bring.

2 Anne remarks, "What one Christian does is his own responsibility, what one Jew does is thrown back at all Jews." Have the class discuss the validity of this statement. What are some key examples supporting both parts of the statement? Is there any evidence to contradict it?

3 Ask the students to research the importance of D-Day. Check out books on World War II and let the students find information that explains why the Franks believed the war would soon be over. Make a bulletin board about D-Day. Display pictures, charts, information and maps about the invasion.

4 Show a video about the events surrounding the most important day of World War II. Invite someone who fought in World War II and ask him to share his memories of that day.

LESSON 19 — JUNE 13 – AUGUST 1, 1944

Anne celebrates her fifteenth birthday. The invasion is going well, and the Allied forces are making progress every day. Anne reports that an assassination attempt was made on Hitler's life. Anne's entries address more philosophical questions. She has grown more serious in the past few weeks, and this is reflected in her writing.

1 Assign and discuss the reading of this final section. Help students understand that there was no planned conclusion to Anne's diary. Rather, she makes an entry as usual and hides her diary. Unfortunately, she and her family are captured and imprisoned. All but the father, Otto Frank, perished before the end of the War.

2 Discuss with the class how Anne's attitude has changed since the invasion. She is spending more time thinking and less time interacting with others. Why would this be? Is this typical of any emergency situation? Do these types of situations cause people to withdraw into themselves? After one discussion with Peter, Anne is upset over his attitude about earning "easy money" after the war. She wants him to have a purpose in his life. What type of attitude is she looking for in Peter? What does she want him to have or be?

3 Ask a girl to read Anne's final letter aloud. What is contained in this letter that is especially relevant to our lives? It is ironic that in this last letter she reveals so much about herself.

4 Anne often mentions how she never really appreciated nature until it was taken from her. Conduct a short class outside and then have the students focus on things that they would miss if they were forced into hiding.

5 Re-read the Afterword and discuss what happened to the Franks, Van Daans and Mr. Dussel after they were arrested. What happened in the actual war after the Secret Annexe was discovered? Complete the class timeline showing events of the book in relation to the events of World War II.

6 In her last entry Anne says that, if there weren't any other people in the world, she would be a better person. Ask and discuss the following questions: What does she mean by this, and do you agree? What would be her reasoning for this statement? Do you think this is an accurate opinion? Do difficulties make, or simply reveal, a person's true character?

7 Refer to Anne's description of herself as a "little bundle of contradictions." Let students suggest why this was true and give examples from her diary. Discuss some of the important life lessons students have learned from the book.

8 Conclude various assignments and projects, including students' diaries.

9 Evaluate knowledge and skills achieved by students using some of the following options.

1) Assign an essay based on ten significant events of the book, descriptions of the main characters or tracing Anne's maturity.

2) Grade one or more of the assignments completed during the unit.

3) Grade students' diary entries on the basis of their thoughtfulness and completeness.

4) Administer **Master 19.1** and **19.2** as presented or use them as a test bank from which to select and modify items for a quiz you develop.

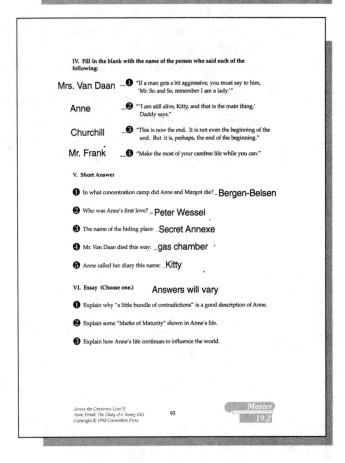

Enrichment

1 Visit a World War II museum, Holocaust center or a Jewish cultural center to build background information to assist the class in understanding the historical period.

2 Have students write their own autobiographies as the book is read. Ask the students to include photographs and/or illustrations. Some students will enjoy making an oral history video or audiotape to share with classmates.

3 Invite an Holocaust survivor or a WWII historian to speak to the class. Encourage students to prepare interview questions.

4 Invite artistic students to build a model of the Secret Annexe, given the information and drawings in the section entitled "July 9, 1942."

5 Read portions of Corrie Ten Boom's *The Hiding Place* to the class. If the movie version is to be used, be careful to preview it first. The graphic nature of certain scenes may be considered inappropriate for the age level of the students.

6 This time period predates television, and people greatly depended on radios. From the local library, check out audiotapes of radio shows of that period. As the students listen, let them evaluate which shows might be popular today. Examples of these shows are: *The Shadow, The Lone Ranger, Jack Benny, Fibber McGee and Molly, Charlie Chan, The Green Hornet* and *Dick Tracy*.

7 Another famous radio show that emphasized the fears and uneasiness of Americans in the late 1930's was Orson Welles' *War of the Worlds*. Share this radio show with the students and let them analyze why the broadcast created such an immense public expression of fear.

Anne Frank: The Diary of a Young Girl

 VOCABULARY LIST

June 14, 1942–March 10, 1943

blithe
allot
ponder
superfluous
annex
satchel
codeine
phenomenon
piqued
barbarism
precaution
saboteur
plied
ration
mince

January 24, 1944–April 14, 1944

perceptive
furbelows
rummage
oblige
inferior
overwhelm
ample
gaiety
nonchalance
optimistic
exempt
hospitable
specimen
prudish
disparage

March 12, 1943–January 22, 1944

emancipate
ulcer
crude
wanton
petrify
trifling
tumult
coquetry
pedantic
irrevocable
capitulate
pursed
oppressive
virtue
stifle

April 15, 1944 – August 1, 1944

scandalous
pseudonym
jocular
upheaval
prefabricated
contrary
boisterous
swindle
coherent
infuriating
muffle
cognac
insurmountable
incessantly
dignitary

Across the Centuries: Level E:
Anne Frank: The Diary of a Young Girl
Copyright © 1998 Convention Press

77

Anne Frank: The Diary of a Young Girl

AMSTERDAM ARCHITECTURE

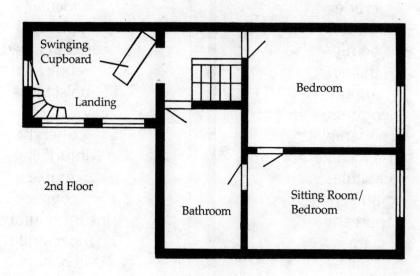

Anne Frank: The Diary of a Young Girl

WORLD WAR II BLACKOUT CURTAINS

❶ The students will collect odd pieces of material and bring them to class.

❷ The classroom windows will be measured.

❸ Groups of three or four will perform tasks: cutting, piecing, stitching, hanging.

❹ The cutting group will cut pieces of material into even shapes.

❺ The piecing group will put the material together with straight pins.

❻ The stitching group will stitch the material so that it is straight.

❼ The hanging group will decide on a creative way to hang the material on the windows.

❽ The curtains may remain up for the duration of the book.

Across the Centuries: Level E:
Anne Frank: The Diary of a Young Girl
Copyright © 1998 Convention Press

Master 2.2

Anne Frank: The Diary of a Young Girl

CHANUKAH WEB

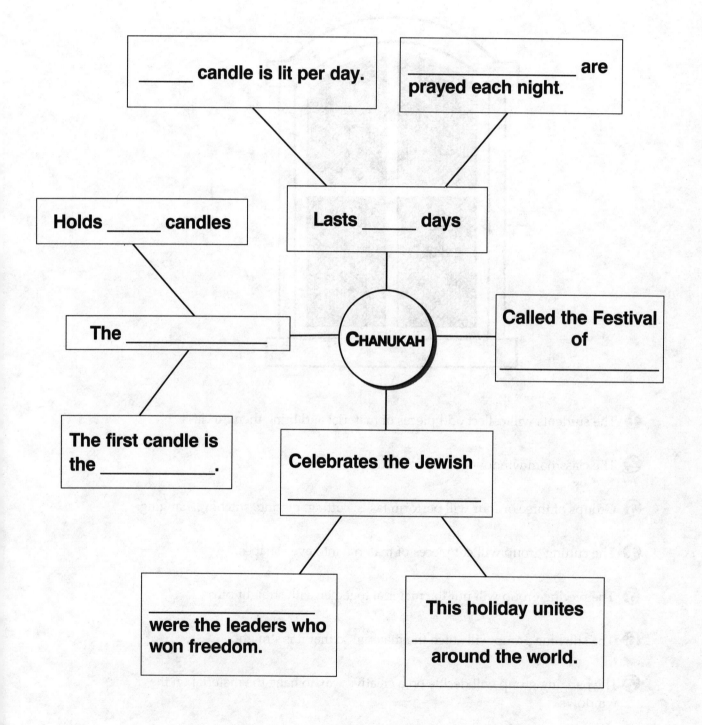

Across the Centuries: Level E:
Anne Frank: The Diary of a Young Girl
Copyright © 1998 Convention Press

Master 5.1a

Anne Frank: The Diary of a Young Girl

St. Nicholas' Day Web

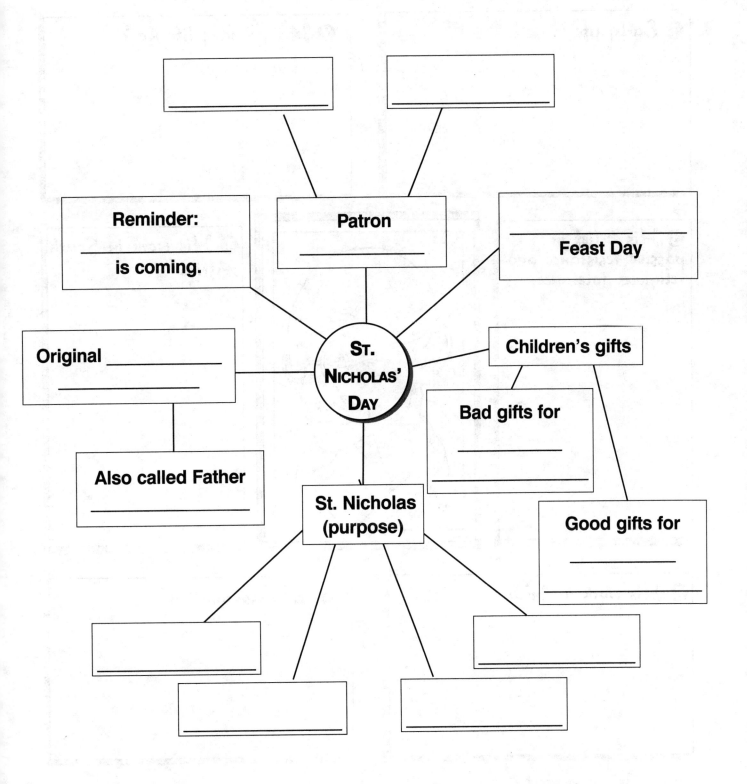

Across the Centuries: Level E:
Anne Frank: The Diary of a Young Girl
Copyright © 1998 Convention Press

Master
5.1b

Anne Frank: The Diary of a Young Girl

RESEARCH NOTES – GANDHI

❶ Early life

❷ His primary life work

❸ His belief in passive resistance and religious tolerance

❹ His work in South Africa

❺ His work in India

❻ His assassination

Anne Frank: The Diary of a Young Girl

DREIDEL, DREIDEL

Shin, Hey, Gimel, Nun
"A Great Miracle Happened There"

A dreidel is a four-sided top with a Hebrew letter on each side. It is a well-known toy that symbolizes Chanukah. Make a dreidel by decorating and assembling the pattern provided. Demonstrate a game by making rules for each side and using a pile of raisins or pennies. For example, Hey could mean "Take 3 tokens." Nun could mean "Miss a turn."

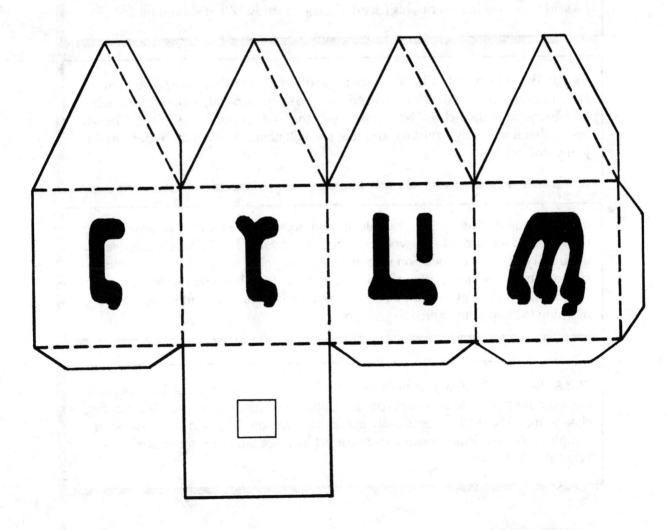

Across the Centuries: Level E:
Anne Frank: The Diary of a Young Girl
Copyright © 1998 Convention Press

Master 5.3

Anne Frank: The Diary of a Young Girl

 **CONFLICT RESOLUTION**

Skit 1: Mary forgot to do her science homework, but she knows that Michael always has his done before school. Without asking him, she takes the completed homework from his book and copies it quickly. She then turns her homework in to the teacher. The next day, the teacher asks her and Michael to stay after class. When the teacher asks them if they copied one another, Michael has no idea what she is talking about. What does Mary do?

Skit 2: Jeff really wants to go to a party that he knows his parents wouldn't approve. In fact, they have already told him that he can't hang out with this group of friends. On the night of the party, his grandma is babysitting him and his sister because his parents will be out for the evening. His grandma would trust him if he said he was going over to his friend's house to study. What should he do?

Skit 3: When Jenny told Cheryl a secret, she did not want Cheryl to tell anyone else. Cheryl "accidentally" slipped and told the secret to another close friend who told everyone in their class. Now Jenny feels that she cannot trust Cheryl. Cheryl insists that it was only a mistake and that she will never do it again. What should Jenny do?

Skit 4: Because of his sports schedule, Joseph doesn't have much time anymore on the weekend for himself. So, when Sunday rolls around, he often feels like sleeping in. Trying to teach their son responsibility, Joseph's parents have left the decision of whether or not to attend church up to him. Joseph enjoys his Sunday school class, and he even enjoys listening to the pastor preach. But is his one morning to sleep in too much to give up?

Skit 5: Brad totally disagrees with the way that his math teacher has been presenting a certain topic. He is always confused, and he is sure that everyone else in the class is, too. The teacher continually makes mistakes on the board while working sample problems. Brad would love to correct him just once in front of everyone. What should he do?

Anne Frank: The Diary of a Young Girl

THE HOLOCAUST

❶ What does holocaust mean? _____
_____

❷ How many Jews were annihilated? _____
_____

❸ What types of laws were made against the Jews? _____
_____
_____

❹ What is the Kristallnacht? _____
_____

❺ How were Jews treated when they were forced to live in ghettos?
_____
_____

❻ What happened in concentration camps? _____
_____
_____

❼ How can we be sure that an atrocity like the Holocaust never occurs again?
_____
_____

❽ What resources did you use? _____
_____

Anne Frank: The Diary of a Young Girl

 CHARACTERISTICS OF FRIENDS

Using the descriptions below, which type of friend would you choose?

MALE

_____ Bobby is the typical football player who is not too bright in the classroom but lives for the sport which he plays. He is a good listener but has to be tough to keep up his image.

_____ Daniel is a straight A student who is not too concerned with whom he impresses. He belongs to the science and math clubs and will probably graduate as valedictorian.

_____ Rob is a romantic. He loves to write poetry, and he also appreciates classical music and drama. He only has one or two close friends, and his dream in life is to be a novelist.

_____ Jordan is the best-dressed guy in school. He is always well-groomed and takes special pride in his appearance. He does not like to get dirty, and he enjoys playing golf. He is intelligent and dreams of being a lawyer.

_____ Eric is a talented musician who enjoys singing and playing his saxophone. His primary hobby is listening to his CD's. He enjoys going to parties, but only if they have a decent band.

FEMALE

_____ Erin is the youngest of five siblings. She has grown up climbing trees and playing with cars. She hates to dress up and is not afraid to say exactly what she thinks.

_____ Lauren is a pretty girl whose only goal is to find a husband. She is clueless when friends tell a joke; they always have to explain it to her. She's always laughing, usually at herself.

_____ Angela has an A average and dreams of being a chemical engineer. She is level-headed and wise. She makes decisions carefully and is a faithful friend.

_____ Alicia likes having the attention of the guys in her class. If you have a boyfriend, she will flirt with him, too. She will be your friend until she wants your boyfriend.

_____ Stephanie is co-captain of the cheerleading squad, and she is sugary sweet to everyone she meets. She would never say a mean word about anyone, but you never know what she is really thinking.

Anne Frank: The Diary of a Young Girl

FAMILY TREE

Use the chart below to find out a little more about your family. Ask your parents, grandparents and other relatives for any information that they might add to your research.

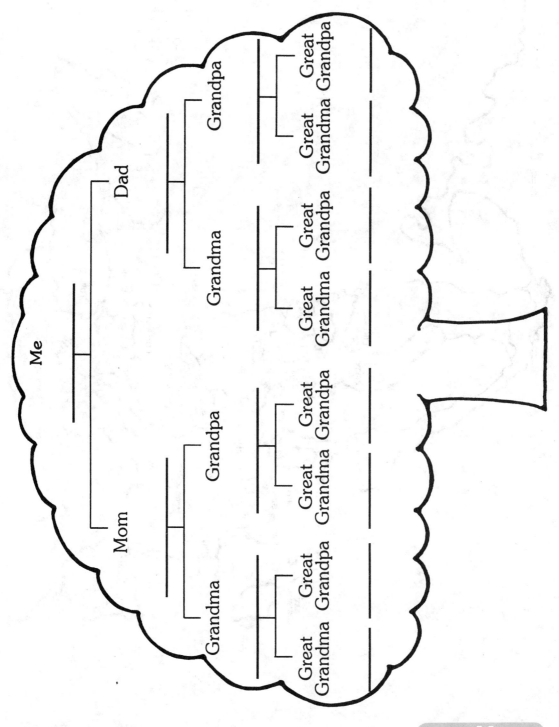

Across the Centuries: Level E:
Anne Frank: The Diary of a Young Girl
Copyright © 1998 Convention Press

Anne Frank: The Diary of a Young Girl
Europe – 1944

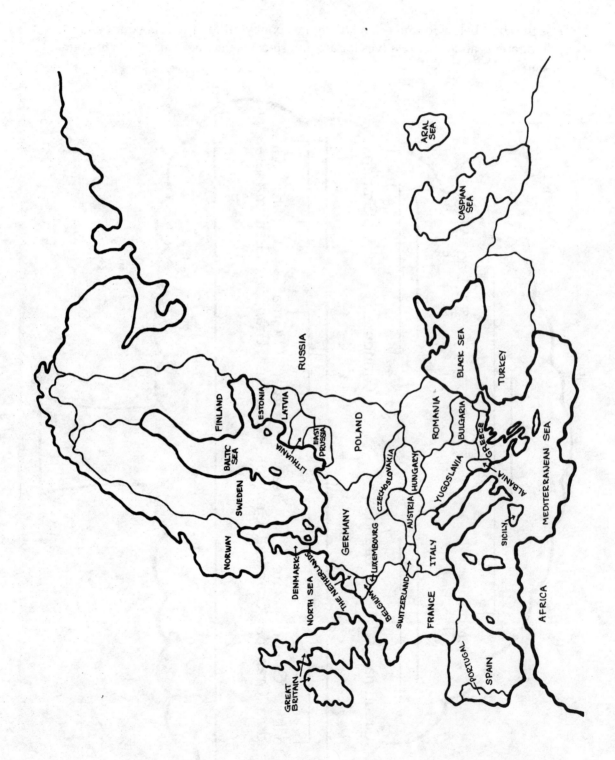

Anne Frank: The Diary of a Young Girl

ANNE'S CHANGES

On March 7, 1944, Anne lists the various changes she believes she has gone through since being in hiding. Are these true changes in her character, or is she just growing up? Think about when these changes would have happened if she wasn't in hiding. Is she growing up too fast, or is she typical of her age?

THEN	NOW
A flirt	
Always getting attention	
Wanted followers	
Felt emptiness inside	
A child	
Content with girlfriends	
"Miss Chatterbox"	
Superficial and lighthearted	

Across the Centuries: Level E:
Anne Frank: The Diary of a Young Girl
Copyright © 1998 Convention Press

Master 13.1

Anne Frank: The Diary of a Young Girl

FAITH AND COURAGE

"He who has the courage and faith will never perish in misery." —Anne Frank

Look up the following Bible verses. In the first column, state what the verse says about faith or courage. In the second column, indicate how well Anne's statement agrees with that verse.

VERSE	MEANING	AGREEMENT?
❶ 2 Chronicles 19:11		
❷ Matthew 9:29		
❸ Ezra 10:4		
❹ Acts 16:5		
❺ Acts 27:22		
❻ Romans 1:12		
❼ 1 Corinthians 16:13		
❽ Joshua 1:7		
❾ Hebrews 11:1		

Across the Centuries: Level E:
Anne Frank: The Diary of a Young Girl
Copyright © 1998 Convention Press

Anne Frank: The Diary of a Young Girl

PRINCESS ELIZABETH

❶ She is Queen Elizabeth II of _____ _____.

❷ Her real name is _____ _____ _____ _____. She is the daughter of King George VI and Queen Elizabeth (the Queen Mother).

❸ Her birthday, _____ _____, _____, is an official holiday in Britain.

❹ She was crowned queen on _____ _____, _____, but she ascended the throne on _____ _____, _____, after her father died.

❺ She is married to _____ _____.

❻ Her official residence is _____ _____ in London.

❼ She has three sons and one daughter: Prince _____, Prince _____, Prince _____ and Princess _____. Prince _____ is in line for the throne. She also has six grandchildren. Prince _____ (Charles' son) is in line for the throne after his father.

❽ Succession passes to the _____ child, either male or female, of the reigning monarch.

❾ Queen Elizabeth can abdicate the throne only with the British _____'s approval.

❿ The Queen's husband is not "_____" Philip because the husband of female monarchs do not have a corresponding title in Great Britain. The wife of a male monarch, however, does take on the title of "_____."

Across the Centuries: Level E:
Anne Frank: The Diary of a Young Girl
Copyright © 1998 Convention Press

Anne Frank: The Diary of a Young Girl

Unit Test

I. Matching: Match the description with the correct person. Some of the answers will be used more than once, and some will not be used at all.

_____ 1. Anne did not get along with this parent.   A. Otto Frank
_____ 2. Tutored Anne daily   B. Mrs. Frank
_____ 3. Liked his cigarettes   C. Anne
_____ 4. Very popular with the girls   D. Margot
_____ 5. Only group member to survive   E. Mr. Van Daan
_____ 6. Would never kiss a boy until engaged   F. Mrs. Van Daan
_____ 7. Supplied food and news   G. Peter
_____ 8. Very studious and smart   H. Mr. Dussel
_____ 9. Oldest Frank daughter   I. Miep
_____ 10. Anne shared her room with this person.

II. Place the following events in chronological order from 1 to 8.

_____ 1. Anne and family were captured.
_____ 2. The family spent its first winter spent in hiding.
_____ 3. Anne died in concentration camp.
_____ 4. Anne fell in love with Peter.
_____ 5. Anne became a woman in her own eyes.
_____ 6. Anne wrote her last diary entry.
_____ 7. The group went into hiding.
_____ 8. Anne received a diary.

III. True/False: Change the false answers so that they are true.

_____ 1. Anne was born in Amsterdam.
_____ 2. Anne died as a result of typhus and starvation.
_____ 3. The story took place during World War II.
_____ 4. Anne didn't like to look out the window because she saw all of the Jews being taken away.
_____ 5. Anne was 16 when she left hiding.

Across the Centuries: Level E:
Anne Frank: The Diary of a Young Girl
Copyright © 1998 Convention Press

IV. Fill in the blank with the name of the person who said each of the following:

_____ ❶ "If a man gets a bit aggressive, you must say to him, 'Mr. So and So, remember I am a lady.'"

_____ ❷ "'I am still alive, Kitty, and that is the main thing,' Daddy says."

_____ ❸ "This is now the end. It is not even the beginning of the end. But it is, perhaps, the end of the beginning."

_____ ❹ "Make the most of your carefree life while you can."

V. Short Answer

❶ In what concentration camp did Anne and Margot die? _____

❷ Who was Anne's first love? _____

❸ The name of the hiding place: _____

❹ Mr. Van Daan died this way: _____

❺ Anne called her diary this name: _____

VI. Essay (Choose one.)

❶ Explain why "a little bundle of contradictions" is a good description of Anne.

❷ Explain some "Marks of Maturity" shown in Anne's life.

❸ Explain how Anne's life continues to influence the world.

TREASURE ISLAND

by Robert Louis Stevenson

INTRODUCTION

Long John Silver, buried treasure and a pirate ship: these are the elements that make an excellent adventure story. Robert Louis Stevenson has combined them into an exciting quest. Since 1883, *Treasure Island* has been the basis for all types of seafaring stories where good meets evil, honor conquers treachery and courage overcomes cowardice. Jim Hawkins, a young boy who only dreams of adventure, becomes entangled with two opposing groups trying to find buried treasure on a tropical island. Caught between such legendary characters as Long John Silver and Captain Flint, Jim fights the final, critical battle for the treasure. Told by a master storyteller, *Treasure Island* is guaranteed to spark the imagination of each reader and to provide a fitting scenario for all children's most daring adventures.

OBJECTIVES:

Treasure Island has often been viewed as a "boy's book." However, as your students read this classic adventure, it becomes clear that there is something in its pages for everyone. From a small sea village to an unknown tropical island, *Treasure Island* is the backdrop for important life lessons such as perseverance, honor, courage, forthrightness and ambition. With distinct representations of good and evil, there is little room for argument as to what is the proper way of living one's life.

1 Students will define and apply to today's challenges the character qualities of honor, courage and forthrightness.

2 Students will compare and contrast the effects of the battle of good vs. evil in *Treasure Island* and give examples from the book of this conflict.

3 Students will describe the seafaring life of the 1700's and what was valued by people during that time period.

4 Students will identify the literary aspects of setting, symbolism, theme, characterization and plot as they relate to the text.

ABOUT THE AUTHOR:

Robert Louis Stevenson lived a relatively short life (1850-1894), but in that time he wrote several literary masterpieces that became the mold for a popular genre today: the adventure story. *Treasure Island*, *Kidnapped* and *The Strange Case of Dr. Jekyll and Mr. Hyde* are only a few of Stevenson's contributions to the art of masterful storytelling. With his thrilling portrayal of treacherous pirates, legendary treasure and a tropical island, Stevenson created a boy's dream world in *Treasure Island*. Stevenson began writing *Treasure Island* for a young acquaintance, and it was first published as a serial in a boy's magazine. Because of his fundamental belief that storytelling is primarily for amusement, Stevenson's stories are replete with fantasy, adventure and romance.

Instructional Plan

Lesson 1 Part One (Chapters 1–3)

Jim Hawkins is a young boy who helps his father keep a small inn, the Admiral Benbow. He remembers clearly the day an old seaman, known as the Captain, took up residence at the inn, claiming he needed a place that people rarely visited. When he drank, he talked about his sea adventures. One day another sailor appears at the inn, and the Captain recognizes the sailor as Black Dog. Following a serious, private discussion, the Captain falls over from a stroke and Dr. Livesey is called. Billy Bones, the Captain's real name, recovers but is still weak. He is frightened of Flint's crew, but he is more terrified of a black spot that will soon be given to him. When it is delivered by a blind man, Billy takes one look, realizes that he only has six hours to live and falls over dead.

1 Master 1.1 provides a list of vocabulary terms that may be new to some students. Provide copies and discuss their knowledge of the various words. They can check dictionaries for the meanings of words that are totally unfamiliar. Assist students in linking new information to more familiar contexts. For example, they can likely describe "the puppy <u>cowered</u> after the gun shot" or "the truck engine needed a complete <u>overhaul</u>."

2 Assign the reading of Chapters 1–3. Direct discussion for students to gain the "big picture" of the section including the main characters, the initial plot development and significant events. Continue discussion on the more finite details. The following questions can assist you in guiding the discussion.

1) What did the old sailor say that he would like to be called? *(Captain)*
2) What was the sailor's scariest story about? *(a man with one leg)*
3) Who threatened the sailor that he had better keep the peace? *(Dr. Livesey)*
4) What was unique about the old man who came looking for the sailor? *(He was missing two fingers.)*

Across the Centuries: Level E:
Treasure Island

5) What was this man's former name? *(Black Dog)*
6) How did Billy Bones, the sailor, get rid of Black Dog? *(He ran him off the property.)*
7) What happened to Billy Bones after he stopped running? *(He had a stroke.)*
8) What is the sign of death to Billy Bones? *(the black spot)*
9) What did Billy Bones say that Black Dog wanted? *(the old sea chest)*
10) After he was given the black spot, how long was he told he would live? *(six hours)*

3 There are few clues given in this chapter as to what is actually to take place, but the reader should be able to pick up enough information to understand that Billy Bones is hiding something from his old crew. As you discuss these introductory chapters with the students, include these key story elements.

1) **Setting**. The students need to know the basic premise of *Treasure Island*—a sea voyage to look for buried treasure. As they are introduced to the first setting of this book, ask why it is important that the Admiral Benbow Inn be located in a sea village. Why is it also important that the inn be secluded?

2) **Symbolism**. Discuss with the class the importance of Billy Bones' song, his adventure stories that do not seem real and the meaning of the black spot.

3) **Theme**. There are three primary themes in the book: good vs. evil, honor vs. treachery, and courage vs. cowardice. Have the students prepare a section for themes in their literature notebooks and then list each theme at the top of a page. Whenever an example of one of the themes surfaces, have the students list the example under the appropriate title.

4) **Characterization**. Detailed information appears about the two main characters in this section, Jim Hawkins and Billy Bones. As Billy Bones spends his last hours at the inn, focus on his need for seclusion, his addiction to rum and the seafaring stories that he tells. Why are they important? What do they foreshadow about the rest of the book? Pay special attention to the stories of a one-legged man and Captain Flint's crew. When discussing Jim Hawkins, focus on his temperament, his goals and how he deals with difficult people and situations.

5) **Plot**. Stevenson's stories demand a very detailed plot. It is important that the students understand each event as it takes place. If not, they can easily get lost. Begin to build a story line bulletin board. Have students draw or write short descriptions of the sequence of events found in the first section of the book.

4 There are two crucial encounters in these chapters. The first one is between Black Dog and Billy Bones. The second is between the blind man and Billy Bones. Divide the class into groups of three or four. Have them act out one of these two episodes. What were Black Dog and Billy Bones arguing about? Students should share ideas about a possible dialogue between the two men.

5 When Billy Bones has a stroke, Dr. Livesey revives him by "leeching" or "bleeding" him. This was a popular practice during the 18th century. Have students research this medical practice and answer the questions on **Master 1.2**.

6 Let students choose from the enrichment activities suggested.

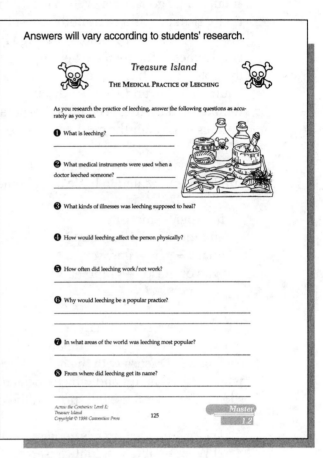

1) Using cardboard or poster board, students can design signs for the Admiral Benbow Inn. What would be an appropriate symbol for the inn? When finished, post the signs around the room.

2) Billy Bones tells many exciting sea adventures. Encourage students to invent stories that Billy Bones could have told about his sailing days.

3) When a production crew prepares to film for a movie, the set designers build models of each scene. Select two students to be movie producers. These students can lead the class in listing on the board important scenes from the first three chapters. Ask student teams to build miniature movie sets. Scenes can be drawn or built as dioramas. Scenes could include the sea village, the Admiral Benbow Inn, the front meeting room and Billy Bones' room.

4) The sea village is similar to hundreds of towns on the Scottish, English, Irish and Welsh coasts. Assign student geographers and artists the project of building 3-D physical relief maps of one of these countries. The teams should paint the physical details and carefully label the more prominent villages and cities.

5) Stevenson was a citizen of the British Empire. At one point in England's history the sun never set on the Empire. Place a world map on the wall. Student researchers and artists can use references to locate and color every country that has ever been a colony of Britain.

Lesson 2 Part One (Chapters 4–6)

After Billy Bones dies, Jim and his mother take the key from around his neck and open the old man's sea chest to find money to pay Bones' bill. They discover a small bag of gold coins. When they hear someone knocking at the door, they hurriedly stuff everything from the chest into a bag and sneak out the back door. They hear the unruly sailors enter the house to discover Billy Bones' body and the empty chest. The men are very upset. It is obvious that they were after more than the gold. Later Jim is questioned and admits he has what the sailors want. The Squire tells Jim and Dr. Livesey about a treasure that is supposedly buried on a remote island. After seeing the treasure map recovered by Jim, the trio quickly decides to go after the gold and jewels.

1 Review new vocabulary terms. Help students apply their knowledge to similar terms related to basic morphemes. For example:

monster — monstrous	Lamentations — lament
ambidextrous — dexterity	sheep — sheepish
guard = gar — garrison	wild — wily
grab or grasp — grapple	duplicate — duplicity (or deduce from the movie title, *Multiplicity*)

2 After reading Chapters 4–6, help students to analyze the character qualities of Dr. Livesey and Squire Trelawney. They are presented as complete opposites to each other. Discuss with the class which character is wise and which is foolish, which one is careful and which one is rash, which one is talkative and which one is silent. Consider these questions in the discussion.

1) How did the Squire's endless talking foreshadow the progress of the trip?
2) What trouble would it cause?
3) Has Jim made any enemies with the sailors who came after Billy Bones?
4) Has the enemy disappeared forever?
5) What will be Jim's role in the adventure?
6) Discuss the fear Jim and his mother faced as they waited for the sailors to leave. Let the class offer personal examples of fearful experiences.

3 Review for specific information based on the following questions.

1) What did Jim's mother ask the neighbors? (*for help to get the sea chest*)
2) How much money was Jim's mother going to take from the chest? (*only enough to pay the bill*)
3) Why did Jim and his mother have to hurry from their house? (*They heard a group of men approaching.*)
4) What was the name of the blind man? (*Pew*)
5) What was a signal of danger for the group of men? (*pistol shots*)
6) To whom did the magistrate take Jim? (*Dr. Livesey*)

7) Whose treasure did the Squire say could be found with the map? *(Captain Flint's)*
8) Where did the Squire go to assemble a boat and crew? *(Bristol)*
9) What was the name of the island to which they would need to travel? *(Skeleton Island)*
10) What position would Jim have on the ship? *(cabin boy)*

4 As individual projects to earn extra credit, let volunteers choose one of the following:

1) What are doubloons, louis d'ors, guineas and pieces of eight? Have students research these items and describe them. In today's money, what would the coins be worth? Encourage students to bring in replicas, drawings or photographs to help the class differentiate between the four types of currency.

2) Present music that was typical of the 18th century. Is there anything that is considered "pirate" music? Let students hear and critique the popular music of this time period.

3) Students can draw treasure maps with yellowed, tattered edges. They should select a scale when drawing distances, such as one inch equals 100 nautical miles. Use the maps to design a bulletin board display.

5 When looking through the chest, Jim wonders why Bones "should have carried about these shells with him in his wandering, guilty, and hunted life." Discuss why Bones held onto some sentimental items and why Jim referred to his life as wandering, guilty and hunted. Bring a chest filled with family heirlooms. As each object is shown to the class, explain the importance of keeping past memories safe.

6 Billy Bones literally died of fright. Invite a guest to share with the class an experience of facing serious illness or an accident or being involved in a war. How did the Lord walk this person through the "valley of the shadow of death"? Do we have to fear death? Why? Why not?

7 Remind students that all people must live with the choices they make. The book of Proverbs explains the outcome for those who choose evil. Let students read and discuss some of the following references in relation to Billy Bones.

- 1:13, 18–19
- 6:12–15
- 11:20–21
- 21:6–7
- 5:21–23
- 10:9–11
- 12:12–13
- 28:17

LESSON 3 PART TWO (CHAPTERS 7–9)

As the chapter opens, Dr. Livesey is in London and Jim is anxiously waiting to hear from the Squire about when they can leave. He finally receives a letter detailing all of the Squire's preparations. They have a boat, a first mate and a one-legged cook named John Silver. It is also obvious that the Squire has been talking a little too much about the treasure. Jim travels to Bristol to join his companions. He wonders to himself whether this one-legged cook could be the same man Billy Bones warned him about. His suspicions are confirmed when he sees Black Dog leaving the tavern. However, Silver pretends not to know Black Dog. Jim is fascinated by the cook and doubts his initial impression. The Squire grudgingly surrenders to the captain's authority, and soon everyone is onboard and the ship is ready to set sail.

1 Let students summarize events to date. The pictures on **Masters 3.1, 3.2** and **3.3** are provided to cue students to significant events.

1) They can be used for students to sequence as they describe events or for each student to draw one from a container and describe a related event. Later, a picture can be passed from one student to another. Students must describe various events related to an individual picture.

2) Provide copies of pictures on which students write questions on one side and answers on the other. These can be used in review activities and as part of the test bank for evaluation purposes.

3) The pictures can be enlarged and used as a background for students to write significant events to be posted in sequence above the chalkboard or on a bulletin board.

2 Let students make predictions about what to expect in the next chapters. Review vocabulary as needed. Assign the reading of Chapters 7–9 and direct discussion of the main events. Compare the characters of Silver and Smollett using the following questions.

1) Why do you think the author has portrayed Silver as the understanding friend and Smollett as the negative troublemaker?
2) Will the characters continue to behave in the same way?
3) Why was Silver working so hard to make everyone like him?
4) Was he succeeding?
5) Were the captain's requests reasonable, or do you think that they had nothing to worry about?
6) Predict what types of trouble the Squire's big mouth is going to cause, even to the point of telling exactly where the island is located.
7) The doctor asked the captain if he fears a mutiny. Are there any signs of potential mutiny?
8) What is a mutiny? Name some famous ones from history.
9) Why did the Squire reveal the secret of the island?

3 Review some of the basic information students need from this section.

1) What was the name of the ship which the Squire had bought? *(Hispaniola)*
2) What was the name of the ship's cook? *(Long John Silver)*
3) Why did Jim give his replacement a hard time? *(He was sad to leave home and his mother.)*
4) Why was Jim sent to see Long John Silver? *(He had a note from the Squire.)*
5) Whom does he think he saw at Silver's tavern? *(Black Dog)*
6) What was Jim's impression of Long John Silver? *(that he was a good sailor and a lot of fun)*
7) Who was the captain of their ship? *(Captain Smollett)*
8) What problems did Smollett have with the voyage? *(There has been much talk. They are going after treasure. He doesn't like his first mate.)*
9) Who has told all of the secrets of the map? *(the Squire)*
10) According to the doctor, who were the two honest men that the Squire had hired? *(Long John Silver and the captain)*

4 Select an activity which will enrich student's learning.

1) Long John Silver is described in detail, as most of the characters are. Assign the students to draw one of the main characters: Jim, Squire, Dr. Livesey, Silver, Billy Bones, Black Dog, Blind Pew or Smollett. Have them use the descriptions from their books for accuracy.

2) Distribute **Master 3.4** and show a video about pirates. Ask the students to write short answers from the information found on the video. Consider the following discussion questions.

1. What were their lifestyles like?
2. What were their morals/values like?
3. What was important to them?
4. Why was this lifestyle glamorous?
5. How does it go against Biblical teaching about a godly, upright lifestyle?
6. Could they be faithful to the Lord and be pirates? Why or why not?

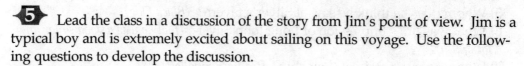

3) These three chapters provide a lot of information about ships and the positions that people hold on the ships. Divide the class into groups and have them each research a different object or position on a ship. Why is it important and what does it do? Let them present their findings to the class.

5 Lead the class in a discussion of the story from Jim's point of view. Jim is a typical boy and is extremely excited about sailing on this voyage. Use the following questions to develop the discussion.

1) What were Jim's expectations for the trip?
2) What experiences would he like to have?
3) How was the voyage the answer to a young man's dreams?
4) Can anyone name other survival adventures? How are these stories similar and/or different from Jim's adventure? (Possible titles would include: *Julie of the Wolves, Hatchet, White Fang, Call It Courage.*)

6 Return to Proverbs to emphasize the danger of talking too much. Let students read and discuss these references.

- 4:24
- 15:2
- 18:6–7
- 13:3
- 17:27–28
- 23:23

LESSON 4 — PART TWO (CHAPTERS 10–12)

The voyage has begun, and even though Jim works very hard, he is still enthralled by everything that happens. The first mate, Mr. Arrow, somehow smuggled alcohol on board and ends up falling overboard one night. Long John Silver is the most beloved sailor on the ship, and the entire crew responds to his orders and advice. However, all of this changes one evening when Jim awakens to voices. One of them is Silver's. As Jim listens, he realizes that there is a major conspiracy taking place on board. After finding the treasure they plan to stage a mutiny in which every honest person will die. Jim reports Silver's plans to the captain, the Squire and the doctor.

1 Review new vocabulary and assign the reading of Chapters 10–12. Return to the suggested development of the plot and complete a listing of sequential events in the story line. Continue discussion with more specific questions and answers. You may want to use the technique of locating specific information. After you ask a question, students must locate the answer in the text, then describe where the information is found rather than the answer itself.

1) What was Silver's nickname? *(Barbecue)*
2) How did Arrow die? *(He fell overboard.)*
3) What was the name of Silver's parrot? *(Captain Flint)*
4) What did the captain think was going to spoil the crew? *(the apple barrel)*
5) What is a "gentleman of fortune"? *(a pirate)*
6) What was Silver trying to convince the young sailor to do? *(join the pirates in mutiny)*
7) Whom did Silver want to kill when they took over the ship? *(Trelawney)*
8) How did Jim know that the map they were using was not the original? *(It was newer paper.)*
9) What was the Squire's suggestion to prevent mutiny? *(blow up the ship)*
10) How many out of 26 men were reliable? *(seven)*

2 An important item for discussion in this chapter is the fact that Jim was listening to a conversation that he shouldn't have heard. Children are taught not to eavesdrop, but in this situation, it seems to be different.

1) Discuss with the students what Jim should have done differently, if anything.
2) What would they have done in his place?
3) Was he wrong to listen in?
4) Was it the only thing he could do?
5) What was Silver's view on money?
6) Why were pirates called "gentlemen of fortune"?
7) What exactly was the pirates' plan?
8) How would they have responded if they had been honest sailors?

3 The Bible teaches that Satan is the father of all lies. He often appears as a smooth talker and someone who wants to be our friend, but he only wants to lead us down the wrong path. Even though Long John Silver is not Satan, he uses a lot of the same techniques to deceive the sailors. By looking at the Bible verses and stories on **Master 4.1**, students can explain what happens in each reference that would agree with how Satan deceives people. Discuss how Christians can stay alert to Satan's lies.

4 In order to find the treasure, the captain had to be able to read a map. Practice with students reading the map on **Master 4.2**. They can answer the questions on **Master 4.3**.

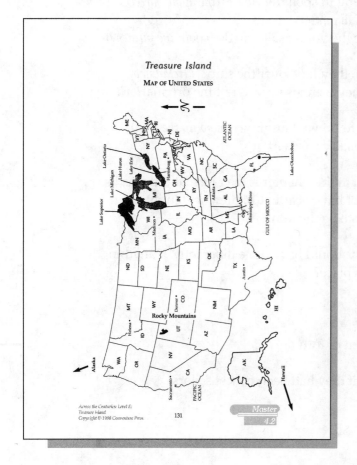

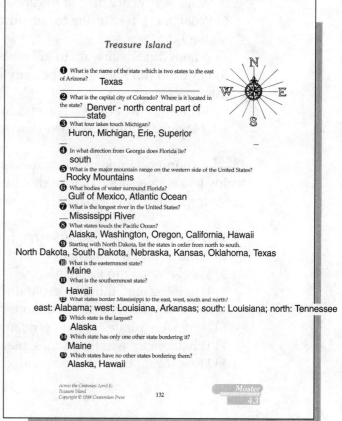

Across the Centuries: Level E:
Treasure Island

5 Discuss what the honest sailors should do in order to stop the pirates? Should they act immediately or wait until they have the treasure? Divide the class into two debate teams. Assign each group one side of the issue: either act <u>now</u> or <u>later</u>. Have the teams list reasons which support their point of view. After approximately 10–15 minutes, begin the debate with this question: When should the honest sailors act? Each group should have an opening statement, at least three different supporting points and a closing statement. When these have been stated, open the floor for questions and arguments. Assign points for each statement, supporting point, question and argument. Then announce which team accumulated the most points. Do not judge the winning argument according to who is more at fault, but which team does the best job of presenting its case.

6 Ask the students to use their writing journals to react to these questions: If you were Jim, or one of the other honest people, what would you want to do about Silver and his men? What do you think is the best plan of action?

LESSON 5   PART THREE (CHAPTERS 13–15)

There are many chores aboard the ship which must be finished before a crew can go ashore. However, amid the complaining, the captain finally agrees to let a landing party embark with Silver as their leader. Six pirates remain on board. The captain, the squire and the doctor are helpless to take command of the ship. When Jim sees that they will not be able to capture the ship, he decides to go ashore. As they approach shore, he jumps out of the boat before they land and runs to hide. Later he witnesses the initial mutiny and retreats into the jungle. There he discovers a man who has been marooned on the island for three years. Ben Gunn is a little crazy, but he is still willing to join Jim's side against the pirates. While they are talking, Jim hears cannon shots and knows that the battle has begun.

1 To review vocabulary for this section, assign pairs of students the task of devising a one- to three-sentence paragraph using a term in context. After each presentation, other students should be able to derive the meaning of the term. For example, "I lay in my berth hoping to fall asleep quickly. However, the cramped space, hard mattress and swaying of the ship made it impossible."

2 Direct students to read Chapters 13–15 and again allow them to list the significant events of the story line. Continue discussion of more detailed information.

1) What was the unique part of Skeleton Island upon which the map was based? *(The Spy-glass)*
2) What did the captain decide to do to calm the nerves of the pirates? *(let them go ahead to the island)*
3) Whom did the captain put in charge of the expedition? *(Long John Silver)*
4) What did Jim witness Silver doing? *(killing Tom Morgan)*
5) Who else was killed while Silver talked to Tom Morgan? *(Alan)*
6) How did Jim react to these things? *(He ran away.)*
7) How long had Ben Gunn been on the island? *(three years)*
8) What food did Ben Gunn ask for? *(cheese)*
9) What happened to the other six men who helped Flint bury the treasure? *(They were killed.)*
10) What did Ben Gunn ask Jim to do for him? *(have one of the people in charge come and talk to him)*

3 The scariest part for Jim is when he sees Long John Silver actually kill someone. Discuss this important turning point with the class.

1) What are the students' feelings concerning the event?
2) What do they think Jim should have done?
3) What other choices did he have?

4) As he ran from the situation, he was saying good-bye to the ship, the captain, the squire and the doctor. How might he have felt?
5) Analyze the personality of Ben Gunn. What was this man like?
6) Had he always been this way?
7) How could he be helpful to Jim and his friends?
8) Did he know anything about the treasure?
9) What was important to him?

4 Let students choose one of the following activities for extra credit.

1) Long John Silver and his men are planning a mutiny or rebellion. Divide the class into teams of three or four. Let each group choose a famous rebellion from history (e.g., American Revolution). This may take some research. Then, after they are familiar with the rebellion, have them act it out in class. Discuss rebellion as a topic with the class. When is it right? What does the Bible say about rebellion?

2) As Jim runs from the boat, he must carefully navigate through trees, swamps and bushes. Plan an obstacle course on your school's field. Divide the class into teams and have a race through the obstacle course.

3) Ben Gunn is a funny man, and many of his lines are quite humorous. Hold a Ben Gunn Impersonation Contest. Let the class vote on the best Ben Gunn.

4) Being marooned on an island seems like a horrible punishment for a sailor. Make a list of the ten most important projects a marooned sailor must accomplish in order to survive.

LESSON 6 — PART FOUR (CHAPTERS 16–18)

With Jim hidden in the jungle, the story narrative is now delivered by Dr. Livesey. He, the captain and the Squire decide how best to protect themselves. They row to shore and find an abandoned stockade. They transport needed supplies, then desert the ship. As they leave the ship, they are shot at by Israel Hands. They make it to shore, but not before the boat has begun to sink and they lose their last load of supplies and guns. After they are in the stockade, they fortify themselves against the approaching pirates. In the initial skirmish, Redruth is killed and the Squire accepts it as his personal responsibility. The fighting continues into the evening. Jim finds his way to the stockade and joins the small group.

1 Introduce the vocabulary for Part Four (Chapters 16–18) by placing the following list of synonyms on the board. The students can use **Master 1.1** to choose and defend the matches.

killed
stubborn / won't let go
small glow from a fire
a large pistol
gun shells
rowed a boat
dishonest person / scoundrel
to flow from high to low
swamp or marsh
one who violently attacks
surround with attackers
great worth
move about / be busy
wrestle / push and shove
large waterproof covering

2 Assign the reading of Chapters 16–18 and lead a general discussion of the events. Continue with a review of more specific information.

1) Who was sent ashore to gather information? *(Dr. Livesey and Hunter)*
2) What was the doctor's first thought when he heard the man being shot? *(that it was Jim Hawkins)*
3) Which sailor did Captain Smollett convince to join him because he knew he was good at heart? *(Abraham Gray)*
4) What position did Israel Hands hold when he was on Captain Flint's boat? *(gunner)*
5) Who was the best shot among the Captain's crew? *(Squire Trelawney)*
6) Of the two sailors left to guard the stockade, which one could not be fully trusted? *(Joyce)*
7) What was Gray's best weapon? *(cutlass)*

8) Which one of the honest sailors was killed during the first battle? *(Tom Redruth)*
9) What did Redruth ask for as he died? *(a prayer to be said)*
10) Because they lost their second load when the boat sank, what did the men in the stockade need? *(rations)*

3 Throughout these chapters, help the students pay special attention to the detailed events which occur. There are several small plot twists which are important to understand. Focus on where the characters are at different times. Look at how they are responding to different circumstances. These chapters provide a lot of insight into the characters' motives and values. Most importantly, the Squire has become guilt-ridden for bringing his friends into such a harmful situation. Whether or not it is his fault is of little consequence. He particularly takes the death of Redruth hard as he feels responsible for any lost life. Focus on the new surroundings of the stockade. Draw a diagram of it for the class to help set the scene.

4 Let students choose an enrichment project.

1) In Chapters 16 and 18, there is a description of the stockade. As a class project or individually, have volunteers build a model of the stockade for display in the classroom.

2) The battle begins in Chapter 17. Have volunteers choose music that they think would be most appropriate for the action in this chapter. It can be from a CD, a television show or a movie, but it must fit the scene. Let them share their chosen music the next day.

3) Squire Trelawney holds himself responsible for the predicament in which his crew finds itself. There are numerous Bible stories where the leader in charge finds himself in a difficult predicament and blames himself for the problems. Assign students to read the Bible stories on **Master 6.1**. Identify the leader, the problem, who is responsible and why. Discuss the answers with the class.

4) Let students complete a writing assignment in their journals: Would it have been better for the heroes to stay on the ship, or would they be safer in the stockade? Defend your reasoning.

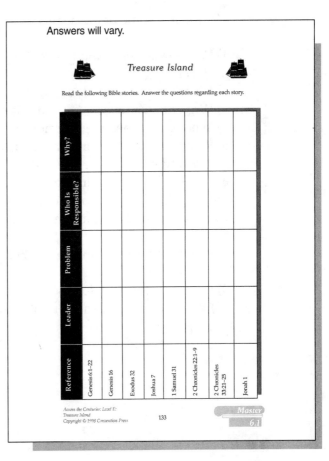

LESSON 7 — PART FOUR (CHAPTERS 19–21)

Jim is the narrator again. When he realizes that his friends are at the stockade, he tells Ben that he must join them. When he tells the doctor about Ben Gunn, Livesey is a little wary but agrees to meet him. During the night, they can hear the pirates singing and laughing. The next morning, a white flag is waved by Silver himself. Long John Silver proposes that, in return for the treasure map, they will be allowed to live. Captain Smollett's response is that all of the pirates must return to face a fair trial in England. Silver stomps away, threatening to attack. It begins an hour later, but the Captain's group claims victory in the end.

1 Review vocabulary as needed and assign the reading. As you lead the discussion, remember that the details in these chapters are very important. Focus on the setting and the themes of honor vs. treachery and courage vs. cowardice.

1) As the students read about the battle, have them decide who has the advantage.
2) Does the stockade have anything that would help the faithful group overcome the difference in numbers?
3) Look for specific examples of both themes.
4) In what ways are the pirates only treacherous and cowardly?
5) Do they also show some positive traits?

2 Review some of the details for this section.

1) Where was Ben Gunn to wait for someone to meet him? *(where Jim found him the first day)*
2) What flag was now flying over the *Hispaniola*? *(the Jolly Roger, the pirate flag)*
3) What did Dr. Livesey carry in his snuff box? *(a piece of Parmesan cheese)*
4) Who approached the stockade carrying the flag of truce? *(Long John Silver)*
5) Where did the captain agree to meet with Long John Silver since he wouldn't be allowed in the stockade? *(outside the fort)*
6) What was Silver asking for from the Captain's men? *(treasure map)*
7) What did Captain Smollett say he would do for the pirates if they would come to the stockade, unarmed, one by one? *(take them back to England for a fair trial)*
8) Why was the Captain angry when he came back into the fort? *(Only Gray was at his post.)*
9) What was Joyce to do if he saw anyone approaching? *(shoot him)*
10) What were the odds after the battle? *(nine pirates to four good men)*

3 Students can choose a project for extra credit.

1) There are now two flags flying over Treasure Island. The first is the British flag, the Union Jack. The other is the Jolly Roger, or the skull and crossbones. Divide the classroom into two camps: the British side and the pirates' side. Make flags on large pieces of material and hang them on the appropriate sides. Decorate the camps and leave the classroom as a battleground until the battle is finished. The class can be divided into two teams to re-enact the battle scenes.

2) Before reading Chapter 20, have the students devise a treaty that could be signed by both sides. What would need to be conceded by both the pirates and Captain Smollett's men? Would there be any chance for agreement after all that has happened?

3) Publish a newscast about the battle. Divide the class into groups of four or five. Let them assign parts within the group. Each newscast should include a top story, weather predictions for tomorrow and interviews. Groups should videotape their newscasts to be shown in class.

4 Assign a topic for students to write in their journals: Speculate on why Ben Gunn wants to see one of the people in charge. Does he really have information, or is he just trying to get some good food? Do you think that he has really gone crazy, or is he just pretending?

LESSON 8 — PART FIVE (CHAPTERS 22–24)

After the battle the pirates do not return. Dr. Livesey leaves on a mysterious errand. Jim plans to row to the *Hispaniola*, cut it loose and let it drift to shore ensuring that the pirates cannot leave without them. When he finally cuts through the anchor rope, the ship speeds toward shore, carrying Jim and his boat along with it. The next morning, he is surprised to see the *Hispaniola* tossing on the waves with no apparent direction. Jim decides to reclaim the ship.

1 Introduce the vocabulary for Part Five. Let students look at their list on **Master 1.1**. Quickly pair them to share information on any known terms. Regroup them by fours and repeat the process. Let groups tell you the terms for which they have no clues. Let other groups share information on terms. Finally, let volunteers check dictionaries for remaining terms.

2 After students have read Chapters 22–24, discuss the major events and motivations of the characters. The primary theme in these chapters is courage. Jim's true character is seen, and he is obviously not always wise and cautious. However, he is courageous and proves it many times. Discuss with the class Jim's accomplishments, then determine if he was really courageous or just lucky. Do students think that the events could really happen, or was it just a part of this fantasy? Focus on how Jim handles fear during these episodes. His fright provides some reality to the chapters.

3 The following questions relate to more specific details of this section. Review and discuss them as desired.

1) Where did Jim think Dr. Livesey had gone in the middle of the afternoon? (*to see Ben Gunn*)
2) What did Jim take with him in order to keep from starving? (*biscuits*)
3) What was Jim going to look for when he left the stockade? (*Ben Gunn's boat*)
4) Once Jim had the boat, what was his goal? (*to cut loose the Hispaniola*)
5) Whom did Jim hear arguing on the ship? (*Israel Hands and the man in the red stocking cap*)
6) What happened to Jim's little boat when the *Hispaniola* started drifting to shore? (*It was carried along with it.*)
7) As he slept out on the sea, what did Jim dream of? (*home and the Admiral Benbow Inn*)
8) What kind of animals did Jim see on the far side of the island? (*sea lions*)
9) What two possible options did Jim think had happened to the sailors onboard the ship? (*that they were either drunk or had deserted the ship*)
10) What was the worst thing the ship could do while Jim was trying to get onboard? (*stand still*)

4 If you live close to a lake where rowboats can be rented, take a field trip. Jim found Ben Gunn's rather small boat and had to row himself to the *Hispaniola*. Let students learn how to row. They can take turns, in pairs, learning how to work together to row their boats. Make sure that all safety precautions are taken, but enjoy the day outdoors as the class learns a skill that Jim had to learn.

5 In groups of two, one for each character, direct students to write dialogue for the argument between Israel Hands and the other sailor as if it were a play with assigned lines. What are they arguing about? Who is winning?

6 Several times throughout this section, Jim is faced with extreme fear which could cause him to give up. Using **Master 8.1**, let students work in groups to look up verses related to fear. They can discuss God's promises. What does this mean for them when they are frightened?

7 Direct the students to answer this question in their journals: If you were Jim, what event would have been the scariest for you (and why)?

1) untying the ship so that it drifts to shore
2) peeking in the window at the argument
3) being carried along by the *Hispaniola*
3) not knowing where to land the boat
4) taking control of the boat by yourself

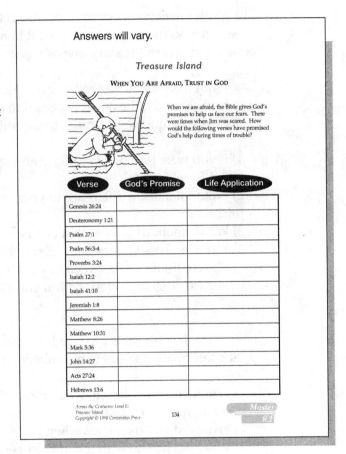

LESSON 9 PART FIVE (CHAPTERS 25–27)

Jim takes control of the *Hispaniola* and finds Israel Hands. They agree to sail the ship together. However, Hands plans to kill Jim later. As they anchor the ship, Jim senses Hands approaching with a knife. A struggle ensues, with Jim almost hit by the knife. Just as Hands throws his weapon, Jim shoots his pistols and Hands falls overboard. Jim then goes ashore to join his comrades. When he reaches the stockade, he realizes that the fort has been overtaken by the pirates.

1 After reviewing vocabulary, assign the reading of Chapters 25–27. Because the action is so riveting you may want to read sections aloud in class. Continue to sequence events in the story line as students identify and discuss them.

2 Jim has been acting rather courageously lately, but in these chapters he does something that he never expected to do: kill a man. Discuss this event with students, using questions similar to the following.

1) If you were Jim, what would your feelings be when you realize that you have killed Israel Hands?
2) Would it make a difference in your mind if it were self-defense, as it was for Jim?
3) What emotions do you think he is experiencing?
4) What bothers you the most about this episode?
5) The confrontation between Jim and Hands is a good example of the theme of honor vs. treachery. How do Jim and Hands exemplify these two characteristics?

3 Use the questions provided as students discuss major events in which more specific information needs to be embedded.

1) When Jim got onboard, what appeared to have happened to the two sailors? *(They appeared to be dead.)*
2) What did Hands ask for when he finally awoke? *(brandy)*
3) What did Jim do with the Jolly Roger? *(threw it overboard)*
4) What was the bargain that Jim made with Israel Hands? *(If Jim gave him food, drink, and a scarf to tie up his wound, Israel would sail the ship for him.)*
5) When Jim pretended to get wine for Hands, what did he see Hands do? *(get a knife to kill Jim)*
6) How long had Israel Hands lived on the seas? *(30 years)*
7) How did Jim kill Hands? *(Jim shot him.)*
8) What did Jim do with the pirate wearing a red stocking cap? *(threw him overboard)*
9) What did Jim hope would make Captain Smollett forgive him for running away? *(capturing the ship)*
10) When Jim got back to the stockade, who was now in control? *(Long John Silver and the pirates)*

Across the Centuries: Level E:
Treasure Island

4 To describe an intense battle scene, an author must use an array of verbs and adjectives to convey the action and related emotions. During reading or as a review, these can be listed on the board and later used in original sentences as students practice the technique of producing "high drama" in the minds of the readers. They can also use the vocabulary in describing a dramatic adventure scene from a familiar movie or TV program.

5 The students can design a comic strip with part of the dialogue between Jim and Hands. They can color, laminate and display these around the room for others to read.

LESSON 10 — PART SIX (CHAPTERS 28–30)

The pirates capture Jim and he is forced to make a choice between joining them or staying faithful to his friends. Jim refuses to join the mutiny. The other pirates want to revolt against Long John Silver and are ready to give Silver the "black spot." The next morning the doctor comes to visit. When he sees that Jim has come back, he asks to speak to the boy alone. Silver makes Jim promise not to run away. When the doctor learns what Jim has accomplished, he is proud of Jim's efforts. The doctor promises Silver to do all that he can to save Silver's life after they return to England.

1 Discuss the final section of new vocabulary listed on **Master 1.1**. Again lead students in discovering known information from which they can derive new meanings. For example:

loop + hole → a way to escape from a convoluted or difficult situation
pale (pole) or impale → palisade
man / manage / manual / manipulate → maneuver
sign / signal → ensign

2 After students read Chapters 28–30, discuss the important changes that occur in this section.

1) Long John Silver appeared to have suddenly changed from being a villain to a hero. What caused this change?
2) How does this change students' character analysis of Silver?
3) Do they think that he was sincere?
4) Were Jim and the doctor stupid for supporting him in this change?
5) Were the pirates' grievances against Long John Silver reasonable ones, or were they just upset with their leader?
6) How did Silver respond to them?
7) Were his replies logical?
8) Focus on the doctor's visit to Jim. Where had the faithful sailors gone?
9) What appears to have happened?
10) Was there any hope of Jim joining his friends again?

3 As students discuss major events, let them also identify specific information in the lesson.

1) How many pirates were there? *(six)*
2) What did Silver say was the opinion of the honest sailors about Jim since he ran away? *(They had written him off; thought he didn't exist.)*
3) For what reason were the five pirates having a meeting outside? *(whether or not to continue following Long John Silver)*
4) What deal did Silver make with Jim? *(They would look out for each other.)*

5) Where did the pirates get the black spot that they gave to Silver? (*They cut it out of a Bible.*)
6) When it came to a vote, whom did the pirates elect as captain? (*Silver*)
7) What did the doctor say was wrong with the pirate named Dick? (*fever*)
8) What did Silver make Jim promise when he went to talk to the doctor? (*not to run off*)
9) What did the doctor promise to do for Silver if they ever got home? (*to try to save him from perjury*)
10) What bothered Jim about his friends' disappearance? (*There was no explanation for their deserting the stockade.*)

4 Let students choose an enrichment activity for extra credit.

1) Like Long John Silver, there were many people in the Bible who changed from bad to good apparently overnight. After reading the Bible stories on **Master 10.1**, students can list how each individual changed, why he or she changed and what was a result of the change.

2) When the pirates gave Long John Silver the black spot, in effect they put him on trial. Hold a mock trial for Long John Silver. Appoint a judge, lawyers, witnesses, etc., and decide whether or not Silver deserves punishment.

3) Jim kept his word to Long John Silver about not escaping when it appeared that Silver's only purpose was to harm Jim. Using the Bible for support, direct students to explain why Jim was right in doing this. They can write a one- or two-page essay to relate this action to Jim's character.

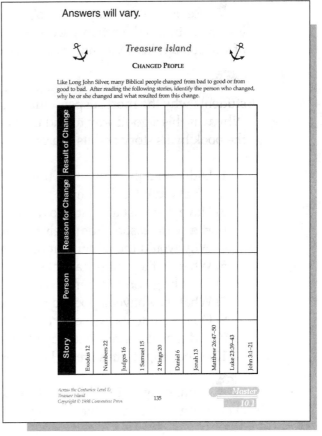

5 Discuss the following questions with the class, then encourage them to write their reactions in their journals: If you were Jim, would you believe Silver's change of heart, or would you still not trust him? Why?

LESSON 11 PART SIX (CHAPTERS 31–34)

Using the copy of the map, the pirates explore the island in hopes of finding the treasure. The pirates freeze when they hear an eerie sound, and Silver realizes it is Ben Gunn's voice. When they reach the spot where the treasure should be, it has disappeared. The pirates quickly take sides against Silver and Jim. Three shots ring out and the pirates run away. The doctor, Ben Gunn and Gray emerge from the trees. Ben Gunn has hidden the treasure in a cave. The men put the treasure onboard the ship and sail for England, leaving three rebellious pirates marooned on the island. Silver takes one sack of the gold and escapes in an extra boat, never to be seen again.

1 Review vocabulary and assign the reading of Chapters 31–34. Because this lesson continues the action-packed adventure leading to the climax and resolution of various conflicts, you may want students to read aloud various portions in class.

2 A climactic ending is fitting for the Stevenson adventure. Discuss with the students why the most suspenseful part of the book has been saved for the end. Why was this a good way to end the book? When finished, have them evaluate the book by its story and its characters.

1) Did it hold their attention until the very end?
2) What did it teach them?
3) Have them list at least two things that they learned from the book and support it with reasons from their reading.
4) Why would the faithful group be glad to be rid of Long John Silver?
5) What do they think happens to Silver?
6) Does he go on to other adventures?
7) What may have happened to the marooned pirates?
8) Do the students feel sorry for them?
9) Did they deserve what they received as their punishment?
10) What might Jim's life be like after returning home?

3 Embed questions of specific information as students discuss the major events and add them to the story line.

1) Whose body of bones did the pirates find as they were searching for the treasure? *(one of Flint's men, Allardyce)*
2) What was Flint's only song? *("Fifteen Men")*
3) When the pirates first heard the mysterious voice, who did they think it was? *(Flint's ghost)*

4) What did the pirates say about how harmless Ben Gunn was? *("Nobody minds Ben Gunn.")*
5) When they found the treasure location, what did they discover? *(It was gone.)*
6) Who fired shots on the pirates? *(the doctor, Ben Gunn and Gray)*
7) Where did they find the squire and Captain? *(in Ben Gunn's cave with the treasure)*
8) How did the squire respond to Silver's presence? *(said Silver was a villain, but he would protect Silver)*
9) What happened to the three pirates on the island? *(They were marooned.)*
10) How did Silver escape? *(He took a bag of gold and sailed off in an extra boat during the middle of the night.)*

4 Let students volunteer for an enrichment activity.

1) Plan a treasure hunt for the class. Give them clues that they must decipher in order to find the "treasure." Divided into teams, this can be an excellent group activity.

2) Assign students to write the events of the last four chapters in a newspaper article format. Have them relate the events in a "who, where, when, why, how" format. There should be no editorializing or dramatic language in their articles.

3) Divide the class into groups. Have them choose their favorite part of the book and make a video of it. They can choose any chapter or section they want, but everyone on the team must take part in the video production.

5 Have students write in their journals their reactions to the following questions: What happened to Jim after he returned home? What did he do with his money? Was he content to just stay at home after this adventure?

6 Use the story line students have developed during their discussions of the book to help the students extend their understanding of its internal structure.

1) Relate items to the development of the setting, characters, plot and themes.
2) Let students "chunk" events to state the six or seven major transitions.
3) Direct students to write a summary of the book based on the major events.

7 Provide an evaluation of the unit using one or more of the options suggested.

1) Let students order and describe the major events of the book.

2) Develop a test or project which more accurately reflects your emphases in teaching the unit. The test provided and the various questions in each lesson can serve as a test bank.

3) Provide copies of **Master 11.1a** and **11.1b** for students to complete.

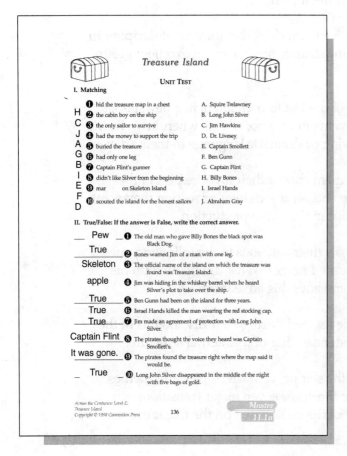
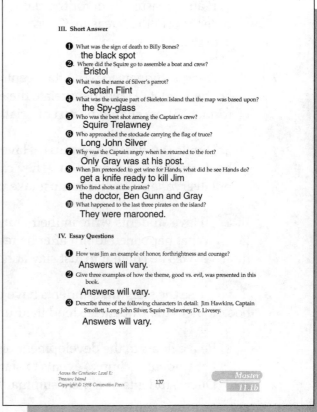

ENRICHMENT

1 Research the subject of pirates in the 1700's and 1800's. What were the lifestyles like? How did they become pirates? What was their main goal?

2 A lot of the book takes place on the *Hispaniola*. Using what is known about the ship, have the students build a model of the ship. Emphasize that the model should be built to scale.

3 There are several film versions of this story. After the class finishes reading the book, show one of the films. Let students compare the book to the film.

4 The characters in this book are very clearly described, both how they look and how they act. Have a class party where everyone dresses up as one of the characters. Give prizes for the most original and most detailed costumes.

5 If a local college or theatre group is showing a production of this play, take your class to see it. They can see it before they read the book to get the basic concepts or after the unit as a special treat.

6 Encourage the class to produce their own puppet show or prepare a class production of the play to be performed for the school or for the parents.

7 If the school has access to the Internet, look up *Treasure Island*. List the sites that are found. Other topics to search would be: buried treasure, 18th century ships, pirates and Robert Louis Stevenson. Be sure to monitor all Internet searches.

8 Build a portfolio of student artwork and written work. Encourage each student to produce five to seven pieces from the book: different scenes, characters, etc. Use the portfolios to display their work.

9 Take a field trip to a museum that shows pieces of art, furniture or artifacts from this time period. Have the students write a short report after the trip. An alternative to this activity would be to have the students use cameras to build a photographic safari of the museum.

10 Stevenson begins his book with a poem that is supposed to persuade the hesitant buyer to purchase his book. After they read the book, have the class members write their own poems, trying to convince someone to read this book.

Treasure Island

Vocabulary List

PART ONE:
Chapters 1–6

1. tarry
2. tyranny
3. cutlass
4. bade
5. hoist
6. swab
7. lubber
8. magistrate
9. cowed
10. apoplexy
11. tinder
12. disperse
13. overhaul
14. miscreant
15. ambiguity

PART THREE:
Chapters 13–15

1. configuration
2. scour
3. swelter
4. mutiny
5. berth
6. foliage
7. aperture
8. extricate
9. snipe
10. frenzy
11. flitted
12. incongruous
13. interval
14. maroon
15. volley

PART FIVE:
Chapters 22–27

1. loophole
2. palisade
3. resin
4. draughts
5. coracle
6. maneuver
7. incessant
8. summit
9. tiller
10. trundle
11. bulkhead
12. elated
13. helm
14. ensign
15. shroud

PART TWO:
Chapters 7–12

1. brood
2. monstrous
3. lament
4. dexterity
5. sheepish
6. mirth
7. quay
8. garrison
9. schooner
10. wily
11. grapple
12. buccaneer
13. quid
14. duplicity
15. agitate

PART FOUR:
Chapter 16–21

1. bustle
2. musket
3. besiege
4. ammunition
5. invaluable
6. sculled
7. scuffle
8. rogue
9. tarpaulin
10. slew
11. ebb
12. dogged
13. morass
14. ember
15. assailant

PART SIX:
Chapters 28–34

1. daub
2. gallows
3. emissary
4. gibbet
5. environ
6. insubordinate
7. bog
8. ruffian
9. prolong
10. folly
11. bated
12. grovel
13. cache
14. bland
15. sojourn

Across the Centuries: Level E:
Treasure Island
Copyright © 1998 Convention Press

Master 1.1

Treasure Island

THE MEDICAL PRACTICE OF LEECHING

As you research the practice of leeching, answer the following questions as accurately as you can.

❶ What is leeching? _____
_____

❷ What medical instruments were used when a doctor leeched someone? _____
_____

❸ What kinds of illnesses was leeching supposed to heal?
_____

❹ How would leeching affect the person physically?
_____

❺ How often did leeching work/not work?
_____

❻ Why would leeching be a popular practice?
_____
_____

❼ In what areas of the world was leeching most popular?
_____

❽ From where did leeching get its name?
_____
_____

Across the Centuries: Level E:
Treasure Island
Copyright © 1998 Convention Press

Master 1.2

Treasure Island

Across the Centuries: Level E:
Treasure Island
Copyright © 1998 Convention Press

Treasure Island

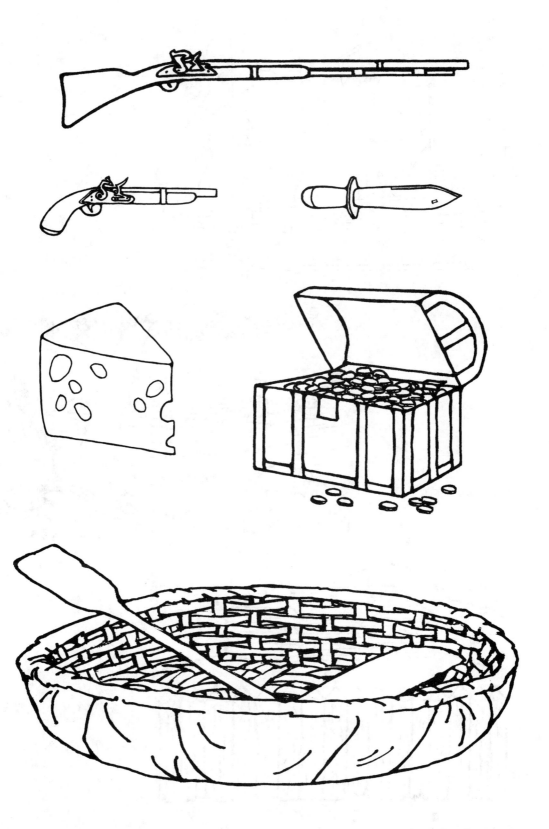

Treasure Island

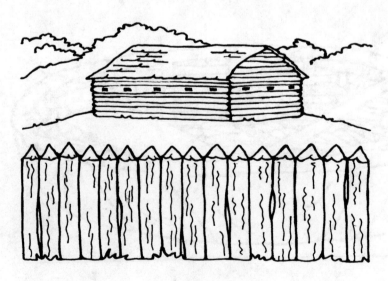

Across the Centuries: Level E:
Treasure Island
Copyright © 1998 Convention Press

 # Treasure Island

PIRATES AND GENTLEMEN OF FORTUNE

❶ What is the definition of piracy?
_____

❷ Where did most piracy take place?
_____

❸ What kind of men owned pirate ships?
_____

❹ How did they capture their treasure?
_____

❺ What countries produced the most pirates?
_____

❻ How did someone become a pirate?
_____

❼ What kind of life did pirates lead?
_____

❽ What did the pirates do with the treasures they captured?
_____

❾ What was the usual punishment if pirates were caught?
_____

❿ Who were the most famous pirates?
_____
_____

Draw your best illustration of a typical pirate.

Across the Centuries: Level E:
Treasure Island
Copyright © 1998 Convention Press

Master 3.4

Treasure Island

LYING AND DECEIT

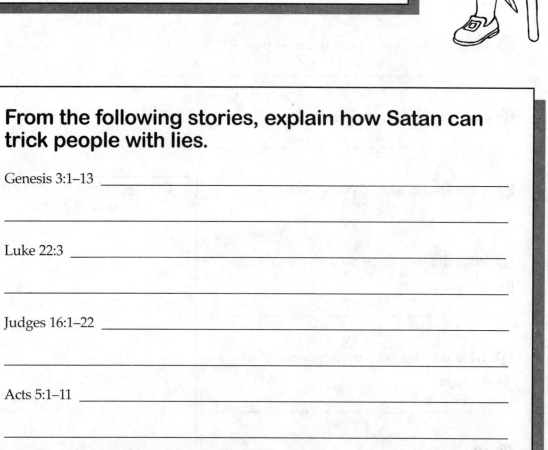

Read the following verses and write how Satan is described as the father of lies.

Mark 4:15 _____

2 Corinthians 11:14 _____

2 Corinthians 12:7 _____

1 Timothy 1:20 _____

John 8:44 _____

From the following stories, explain how Satan can trick people with lies.

Genesis 3:1–13 _____
_____

Luke 22:3 _____
_____

Judges 16:1–22 _____
_____

Acts 5:1–11 _____
_____

Across the Centuries: Level E:
Treasure Island
Copyright © 1998 Convention Press

Master 4.1

Treasure Island

MAP OF UNITED STATES

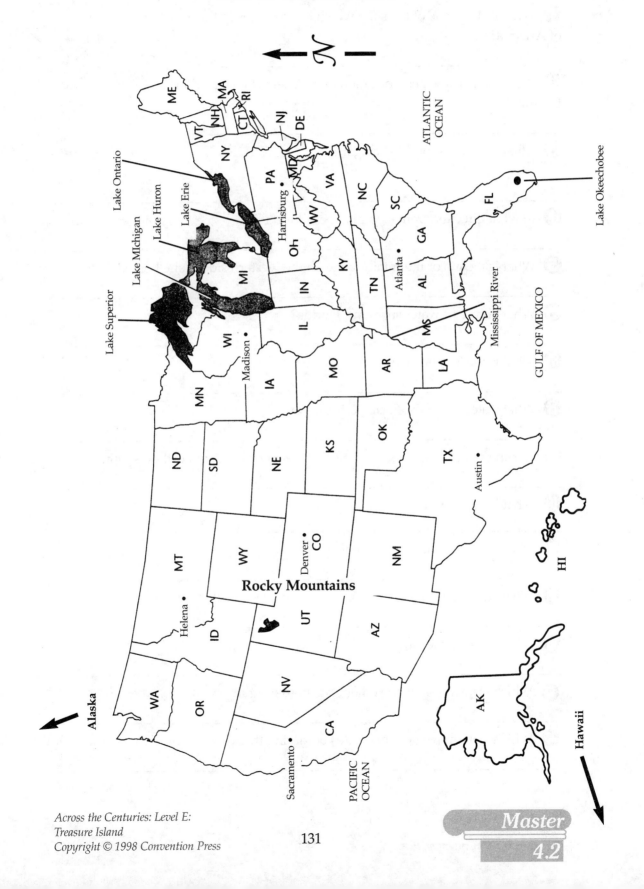

Across the Centuries: Level E:
Treasure Island
Copyright © 1998 Convention Press

131

Master 4.2

Treasure Island

1 What is the name of the state which is two states to the east of Arizona?
_____

2 What is the capital city of Colorado? Where is it located in the state?
_____

3 What four lakes touch Michigan?
_____
_____

4 In what direction from Georgia does Florida lie?
_____

5 What is the major mountain range on the western side of the United States?
_____

6 What bodies of water surround Florida?
_____

7 What is the longest river in the United States?
_____

8 What states touch the Pacific Ocean?
_____

9 Starting with North Dakota, list the states in order from north to south.
_____

10 What is the easternmost state?
_____

11 What is the southernmost state?
_____

12 What states border Mississippi to the east, west, south and north?
_____

13 Which state is the largest?
_____

14 Which state has only one other state bordering it?
_____

15 Which states have no other states bordering them?
_____

Across the Centuries: Level E:
Treasure Island
Copyright © 1998 Convention Press

132

Master 4.3

Treasure Island

Read the following Bible stories. Answer the questions regarding each story.

Reference	Leader	Problem	Who Is Responsible?	Why?
Genesis 6:1–22				
Genesis 16				
Exodus 32				
Joshua 7				
1 Samuel 31				
2 Chronicles 22:1–9				
2 Chronicles 33:21–25				
Jonah 1				

Across the Centuries: Level E:
Treasure Island
Copyright © 1998 Convention Press

Master 6.1

Treasure Island

WHEN YOU ARE AFRAID, TRUST IN GOD

When we are afraid, the Bible gives God's promises to help us face our fears. There were times when Jim was scared. How would the following verses have promised God's help during times of trouble?

Verse	God's Promise	Life Application
Genesis 26:24		
Deuteronomy 1:21		
Psalm 27:1		
Psalm 56:3-4		
Proverbs 3:24		
Isaiah 12:2		
Isaiah 41:10		
Jeremiah 1:8		
Matthew 8:26		
Matthew 10:31		
Mark 5:36		
John 14:27		
Acts 27:24		
Hebrews 13:6		

Across the Centuries: Level E:
Treasure Island
Copyright © 1998 Convention Press

Treasure Island

CHANGED PEOPLE

Like Long John Silver, many Biblical people changed from bad to good or from good to bad. After reading the following stories, identify the person who changed, why he or she changed and what resulted from this change.

Story	Person	Reason for Change	Result of Change
Exodus 12			
Numbers 22			
Judges 16			
1 Samuel 15			
2 Kings 20			
Daniel 6			
Jonah 13			
Matthew 26:47–50			
Luke 23:39–43			
John 3:1–21			

Across the Centuries: Level E:
Treasure Island
Copyright © 1998 Convention Press

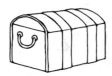

Treasure Island

UNIT TEST

I. Matching

____ 1. hid the treasure map in a chest   A. Squire Trelawney

____ 2. the cabin boy on the ship   B. Long John Silver

____ 3. the only sailor to survive   C. Jim Hawkins

____ 4. had the money to support the trip   D. Dr. Livesey

____ 5. buried the treasure   E. Captain Smollett

____ 6. had only one leg   F. Ben Gunn

____ 7. Captain Flint's gunner   G. Captain Flint

____ 8. didn't like Silver from the beginning H. Billy Bones

____ 9. marooned on Skeleton Island   I. Israel Hands

____ 10. scouted the island for the honest sailors   J. Abraham Gray

II. True/False: If the answer is False, write the correct answer.

_____ 1. The old man who gave Billy Bones the black spot was Black Dog.

_____ 2. Bones warned Jim of a man with one leg.

_____ 3. The official name of the island on which the treasure was found was Treasure Island.

_____ 4. Jim was hiding in the whiskey barrel when he heard Silver's plot to take over the ship.

_____ 5. Ben Gunn had been on the island for three years.

_____ 6. Israel Hands killed the man wearing the red stocking cap.

_____ 7. Jim made an agreement of protection with Long John Silver.

_____ 8. The pirates thought the voice they heard was Captain Smollett's.

_____ 9. The pirates found the treasure right where the map said it would be.

_____ 10. Long John Silver disappeared in the middle of the night with five bags of gold.

Across the Centuries: Level E:
Treasure Island
Copyright © 1998 Convention Press

Master 11.1a

III. Short Answer

1 What was the sign of death to Billy Bones?

2. Where did the Squire go to assemble a boat and crew?

3 What was the name of Silver's parrot?

4 What was the unique part of Skeleton Island that the map was based upon?

5 Who was the best shot among the Captain's crew?

6 Who approached the stockade carrying the flag of truce?

7 Why was the Captain angry when he returned to the fort?

8 When Jim pretended to get wine for Hands, what did he see Hands do?

9 Who fired shots at the pirates?

10 What happened to the last three pirates on the island?

IV. Essay Questions

1 How was Jim an example of honor, forthrightness and courage?

2 Give three examples of how the theme, good vs. evil, was presented in this book.

3 Describe three of the following characters in detail: Jim Hawkins, Captain Smollett, Long John Silver, Squire Trelawney, Dr. Livesey.

ANNE OF GREEN GABLES

by Lucy Maud Montgomery

INTRODUCTION

Since 1908, old and young alike have fallen in love with an unusually talkative, imaginative, red-haired eleven-year-old girl. Anne is an orphan who mistakenly ends up at a farmhouse that expected a boy. She quickly wins the hearts of Matthew and Marilla Cuthbert. The little town of Avonlea on Prince Edward Island is the perfect place for a girl like Anne to get into mischief as many of her fondest dreams come true. As Matthew, Marilla and the rest of Avonlea quickly discover, it is hard to resist Anne of Green Gables.

ABOUT THE AUTHOR:

Probably one of the most beloved children's authors of all time, Lucy Maud Montgomery lived the life which she wrote about in her books. Born on Prince Edward Island and educated in Charlottetown, Montgomery was one of the few women of her time to receive a higher education. She based her stories on the life that she experienced when she returned to Prince Edward Island to teach. *Anne of Green Gables* has been translated into seventeen languages and has been made into numerous movies, plays and television shows. Montgomery has definitely produced, as Mark Twain once said, "the sweetest creation of child life yet written."

OBJECTIVES:

Anne of Green Gables is the story of an unusual young girl. Anne finds herself in so many predicaments that the reader often wonders whether or not she will survive her childhood. Young people easily identify with the young heroine and can learn from her mistakes. Each dilemma is educational for Anne. She never makes the same mistake twice. There are numerous lessons to be learned from Anne's experiences, the most important of which is surviving all the "mess-ups" of life.

1 The students will interpret the values of acceptance, loyalty, self-control and honesty by seeing how Anne deals with different situations and applying them to their own lives.

2 The students will describe Prince Edward Island in the early 1900's and the historical events which are important at that time.

3 The students will identify the theme of friendship in the story by listing the attributes of true friendship in relation to Biblical principles.

4 The students will identify the literary aspects of setting, symbolism, theme, characterization and foreshadowing as they relate to the book's plot.

PREPARATION FOR READING:

1 Select vocabulary activities which will assist the class in understanding new words. **Master I.1** lists a selection of these interesting words. Students can:

1) Build crossword puzzles using selected vocabulary.

2) As teams, devise a lesson to teach ten words to peers or a younger class.

3) Act out the meaning of a word.

4) Build word walls, e.g., large posters that hang from the ceiling. Words, their definitions and illustrations are placed on the word walls.

5) Build web walls, e.g., large sheets of paper displayed around the room. Each web is based on a category. Examples would be parts of speech or archaic vs. modern words. Students categorize their vocabulary lists and add additional words found in the chapters.

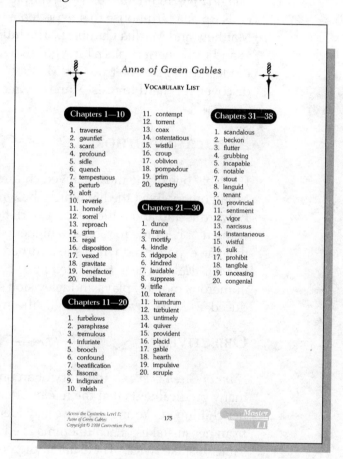

2 Diaries were popular methods of writing in Anne's world. Provide copies of **Master I.2 and I.3** (multiple copies) for students to make a "Green Gables Diary." Divide the diary into sections:
1) Literature Reactions
2) Review Questions
3) Character Analyses
4) Personal Opinions

Plan to use the diaries throughout the unit and consider evaluating it as a part of the final assessment.

3 Ask students to research and report on life as it might have been on Prince Edward Island (or any small community) during the early 1900's. Some questions to include are:
1) How did various people earn a living?
2) What chores and activities were common for young teens?
3) What types of education were common? Were there differences in opportunities for girls and boys?
4) What were the clothing styles?
5) Where and how was the shopping done?
6) What modern conveniences were or were not available: electricity, radio, car, indoor plumbing, phone, television, etc.?
7) What were the modes of transportation?
8) What happened to children who had no family?

4 Consider showing only one short segment from a film of *Anne of Green Gables*. You may want to stop the film just prior to the climax of one of her most exciting capers. Use the episode to introduce the book and heighten curiosity as to the "end of the story." Assure students that you will show the episode again after reading the section in the book.

5 Provide access to other books by Lucy Maud Montgomery.

Anne of Avonlea. Bantam, 1976.
Anne of the Island. Bantam, 1976.
Anne's House of Dreams. Bantam, 1981.
Chronicles of Avonlea. Bantam, 1988.
Emily of New Moon. Bantam, 1983.
Golden Road. Bantam, 1989.
Pat of Silver Bush. Bantam, 1989.
Further Chronicles of Avonlea. Bantam, 1989.

Anne of Ingleside. Bantam, 1981.
Anne of Windy Poplars. Bantam, 1981.
The Blue Castle. Bantam 1989.
Emily Climbs. Bantam, 1983.
Emily's Quest. Bantam, 1983.)
Jane of Lantern Hill. Bantam, 1989.
Tangled Web. Bantam, 1989.

Instructional Plan

Lesson 1 — Chapters 1–2

Mrs. Rachel Lynde is the town busybody. One day she sees Matthew Cuthbert all dressed up and on his way to town. She hurries to Green Gables to ask his sister, Marilla, where he is going. Marilla tells her that she and Matthew are adopting a little boy. However, there is a big surprise awaiting. Instead of bringing a boy, Matthew arrives at home with a little red-haired girl named Anne.

1 Review vocabulary and assign the reading of Chapters 1 and 2. Remind students that, as they enjoy the story, they are to attend to how the author establishes the setting, develops the four main characters in this section, and begins the plot.

2 Discuss the major events of the story line and the parts students found most interesting. Lead the discussion to the initial literary aspects of the book.

1) **Characterization**: Lucy Montgomery was very skilled in her use of descriptive vocabulary and foreshadowing events. Studying some of these descriptive passages will give students a more complete picture of Anne and will increase their own imaginative skills. In very few books are characters given such a complete description as in the "Anne" stories. The reader is supposed to fall completely in love with Anne. Therefore, the author gives a thorough description of the young girl, both her positive and negative qualities. Let the students begin a characterization section in their notebooks, adding both characters and descriptions as the class reads the chapters. Focus on Anne, Matthew, Marilla and Mrs. Lynde in this first section.

2) **Foreshadowing**: This is one of the more important literary aspects in this book used to keep the interest level high. Make sure students identify this component of the story as they read. Have them identify the foreshadowing in each section and then predict what will likely happen next.

3) **Setting**: Avonlea is a quaint little town on Prince Edward Island, Canada. The descriptions of the location make the book more alive for the reader. Research this area and fill the room with pictures or drawings of Anne's home.

4) **Theme**: There are three primary themes in *Anne of Green Gables* which revolve around Anne. The first one is <u>friendship</u>. This is probably the most important to Anne as she has always longed for a bosom friend. Watch for the expectations she has for a friend, the struggles she has with the reality of friendship, and the ultimate joy she experiences when she finds a friendship that will last. Second, Anne is forced to deal with the issue of <u>acceptance</u>. She must not only accept herself and her own faults, but she also must learn to accept the faults of others. From a Biblical standpoint, this is an excellent aspect of the book to teach the students. Last, <u>self-control</u> is an important lesson that Anne is continually trying to learn. Identify the problems Anne has with self-control and show the students how she learns to control herself.

3 As students discuss the sequence of the story, or in a more direct question-answer session, help students note significant details. (See the review section in Lesson 5 for specific questions.)

4 Assign the task to research and present information on orphanages during the early 1900's. Although not as prevalent today, many unwanted children were placed into orphanages during that time. What were the conditions like, how long did they stay there, and why were they placed there? Let the students design a bulleting board to display their discoveries.

5 Anne's lengthy descriptions of the things around her will occur frequently in this book. The students need to learn to appreciate Anne's language and enthusiasm for life. Based on Chapter 2, ask student volunteers to memorize one of Anne's monologues. Encourage them to present the monologues dramatically. Monologues can be presented to the class or a younger group.

6 Forming mental images of a setting or a character is extremely important. Direct students to use a page in their diaries to draw their mental images as you read a section aloud. Let small groups of students compare their drawings. Emphasize that the details provided help a reader form a clearer picture of what was in the author's mind. Let students practice this literary skill.

  1) Have the students draw one of the characters or one of the places described by Anne on her way home from the train station.

  2) Provide scenic pictures to pairs of students. Direct students to write or orally explain descriptions sufficient enough that the partner can recognize or draw the scene.

7 Discuss the following questions, then ask students to write their reactions in their diaries. Marilla admits to Mrs. Lynde that she has had misgivings about adopting a child. What are her reasons for wanting a child around the house? Why would she not want one? Will it be like a son/daughter to her or just hired help? Analyze what type of relationship Marilla will have with this orphan.

LESSON 2   CHAPTERS 3–4

When Matthew takes Anne home, Marilla experiences the surprise of her life. She is very upset over the fact that Anne is not a little boy and adamant that she be taken back. But as Anne describes her trip home, Marilla is astonished at the girl's imagination and the extent of her emotions. After Marilla puts Anne to bed, Matthew admits that he would like for Anne to stay. This is particularly shocking since Matthew normally does not care for girls, especially talkative ones. However, Marilla's mind is made up. After a delightful morning at Green Gables, Anne is forced to pack her few belongings. Marilla prepares to drive her back. She is very aware of Matthew's feelings about keeping Anne.

1 Review vocabulary and list information students will want to learn. Assign the reading of Chapters 3 and 4.

2 Because the characters are still being developed, continue to discuss what makes each person unique. Focus on the relationships between the characters.

1) How do they relate and interact with each other?

2) What is the power struggle that can be identified in these chapters?

3) Who do they think is stronger and more in charge: Marilla or Matthew?

4) Why are they struggling?

5) Who is on each side?

6) Who do you think will win?

7) Does this agree with your opinion of who is stronger?

8) Does Anne go overboard with her imagination? Give some examples.

9) Is it good to be this imaginative and emotional at this age?

10) What kind of occupation would she be good at someday?

3 Discuss with students that everyone's life has valleys and mountains — times of trouble and sadness and times of success and joy. Place the illustration on the board as you talk.

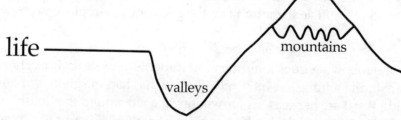

Assign groups to discuss the life experiences of the following Bible characters:
Joseph (Genesis 37, 39)
Ruth (Ruth 1:3–5; 1:16; 2:5–10; 4:13–15)
David (1 Samuel 20: 41–42; 21:10–14; 27:1–2; 2 Samuel 2:3–4)
The Prodigal Son (Luke 15:11–24)

Let students suggest terms from these stories and Anne's experiences to describe the valleys and mountain tops of life. Ask students to share what personal lessons can be learned from this discussion. (*Everyone experiences times of sadness and joy. Either way, they need to trust God to bring good from their circumstances. Time brings healing and change. Our experiences, and others', can help us learn patience and teach us how to comfort others, etc.*)

4 Provide optional assignments for enrichment or extra credit.

1) Anne's imaginative name for herself is Cordelia. Let the students select the most imaginative name that they can for themselves. The name should express who they are or want to be. They can share the names with the class.

2) Anne's description of Avonlea makes the place real for the reader. Divide the class into groups of two or three and have them prepare a travel brochure for the local area. Focus on the tourist sites, points of interest, interesting restaurants, transportation, parks, etc. Why would people want to visit this area? They should make the brochure as colorful and detailed as possible.

3) Anne is quite taken with the flowers at Green Gables and wants several in the house to call her own. Allow students to grow seeds. Each student is responsible for caring for the plants on a day-to-day basis. Chart the plants' growth.

5 Discuss the following question with the class: If Anne were allowed to stay at Green Gables, what good could the characters do for each other? Build a web of possible answers. Ask students to write their predictions in their diaries.

LESSON 3 CHAPTERS 5–6

On their way to White Sands, Marilla asks Anne about her childhood. There is no hiding the fact that Anne had a very sad, difficult past. Both of her parents died when she was a baby. She was taken in twice by neighbors who wanted her to look after their children. Anne was always able to make the best of negative situations. Marilla finds herself pitying the unloved girl. When Marilla learns that Anne is to be sent to care for a stingy and difficult woman, Marilla says that she hasn't completely decided, and she takes Anne home again. Anne is overjoyed at the second chance.

1 Discuss new vocabulary and the information students want to learn. Assign the reading of Chapters 5 and 6.

2 Use the following questions to discuss the chapters.
1) How has Anne's past contributed to her personality?
2) How does Marilla's view of Anne change based on the story she is told?
3) Compare/contrast Anne's first two foster mothers with Mrs. Blewett and Marilla.
4) What are the positive/negative traits of each one?
5) Why is it obvious that Anne is going to be better off with Marilla?
6) Why do you think Marilla is not as tough as she first appears to be?

3 When Marilla allows Anne to return home with her, Anne feels she has been given a second chance. She is determined to improve her behavior and be eternally grateful for this gift. How does this compare with the gift of salvation which God has given to us? What are the similarities in the gift and in our attitude toward the gift? What are the differences? Have the students look up Bible references, including the ones on **Master 3.1**, which will support their opinions on these questions, then discuss them as a class.

4 When Marilla asks Anne to tell her life story, Anne is much more interested in making up a story. Using their diaries, have students write a two- to three-page make-believe life story, ending with sitting in the class today. Ask and discuss: If you could have any story that you want, what would it be?

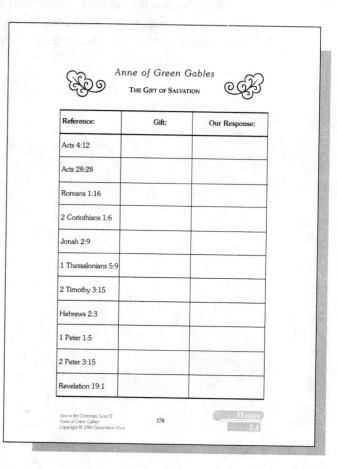

Anne of Green Gables
THE GIFT OF SALVATION

Reference:	Gift:	Our Response:
Acts 4:12		
Acts 28:28		
Romans 1:16		
2 Corinthians 1:6		
Jonah 2:9		
1 Thessalonians 5:9		
2 Timothy 3:15		
Hebrews 2:3		
1 Peter 1:5		
2 Peter 3:15		
Revelation 19:1		

5 Many Christian organizations offer a program to "adopt" a child overseas for a few dollars each month. As a class project, adopt one of these children and continue the project throughout the year. Have monthly "writing days" when students write letters to the child, and collect gifts at Christmas and birthdays to send to the child. Especially allow students to share Christ with this child through letters and drawings.

6 Lead the class in a discussion using the following questions: How should Anne's past experiences make her more accepting and less critical of others? How do they also make her more vulnerable to others' opinions?

 **LESSON 4   CHAPTERS 7–8**

As Marilla puts Anne to bed, she is horrified to discover that Anne never says her prayers and that her image of God is somewhat distorted. The next day, Marilla delays telling Anne that she can stay. Finally, Anne can take it no longer and begs Marilla to let her know the good or bad news. When she learns that she can stay, Anne begins to cry. Marilla decides to have her memorize the Lord's prayer. Anne has a hard time concentrating on the task at hand. The best news that she hears is that she might finally have a friend.

 Title sections on the board as follows:

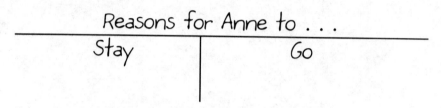

Let students brainstorm and jot their ideas on the board. It will be easier for them to rally to Anne's defense. Challenge them to think through the perfectly good reasons for Anne to go. (*The household would be disrupted. They are old. A boy could help with the chores. A girl can't earn her keep. Girls cost more, etc.*) This will help them appreciate the commitment and sacrifices Marilla and Matthew must make. Discuss vocabulary and assign the reading of Chapters 7 and 8.

Focus the class discussion around the issue of Anne's spiritual development. Marilla is first upset about Anne not knowing her prayers. Discuss what other habits Anne might have that will be upsetting to Marilla. Remember that, in Marilla's eyes, Anne has grown up in an improper environment. How should Marilla deal with this? Discuss Anne's perception of God. How is it correct? How is it incorrect? Is there anything in her perceptions that might be accurate, but most people wouldn't approve of it?

Open a class discussion about prayer. Lead students in pretending that they have never prayed before and have been given the guidelines which Marilla gave to Anne. Ask them to write a prayer based on these guidelines. They do not need to share them in class, but discuss with them that people talk to God in different ways. Let them decide if Anne's prayer was acceptable or if she was off track.

Indicate that Jesus' disciples had the same problems and requested, "Teach us to pray." Distribute copies of **Master 4.1** for students to read and memorize. Remind them that Jesus used this as a model and while it is fine to repeat it in unison, it is really meant to teach us principles about prayer.

1) Recognize and praise God for who He is.

2) Agree to His will.

3) Pray for needs.

4) Pray for forgiveness.

5) Pray for others.

Establish a class prayer list and a daily routine of praying for needs. Record God's answers.

4 Anne falls in love with the beauty of nature around Green Gables. Take a 15–20-minute walk around the school. The students should be quiet as they spend time appreciating the beauty of God's creation. Have them take their diaries and make notes.

5 Anne has very specific requirements for a bosom friend. Using **Master 4.2**, discuss the Biblical concept of friendship. Have students list characteristics that they look for in a friend. Using their ideas, you can build a class web on what makes a friend.

6 Use students' diaries for them to react to the following questions: Anne's idea of God is very consistent with her experiences. How does her view compare with yours? How do you see God?

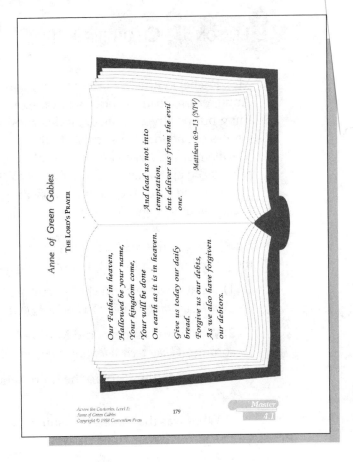

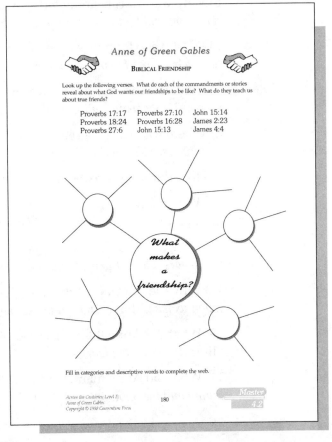

Across the Centuries: Level E:
Anne of Green Gables

LESSON 5   CHAPTERS 9–10

Mrs. Rachel Lynde has not met Anne, so she decides to visit Green Gables. When Anne returns from wandering in the orchard, Mrs. Rachel's comments are anything but positive. Anne explodes and insults Mrs. Rachel, who leaves Green Gables offended. Anne insists that she will never apologize to Mrs. Rachel. Marilla restricts her to her room until she decides to apologize. Finally, Matthew asks her to apologize, and she agrees. When Marilla takes her to Mrs. Rachel's house, Anne gives the most flowery apology anyone has ever heard. Mrs. Rachel accepts it as sincere. Marilla cannot help but laugh at the young girl she is raising.

1   Assign the reading of Chapters 9 and 10 and generally discuss the events of the story line. Continue the discussion as you review Chapters 1 through 10.

1) What made Mrs. Rachel so curious that she had to go and see Marilla? *(Matthew going to town in his best clothes, driving slowly)*

2) What startling news did Marilla have for Mrs. Rachel, and what was her reasoning? *(They were adopting a boy to help Matthew on the farm.)*

3) When Matthew got to the train station, who was waiting for him? *(a little girl)*

4) What was the most astonishing character trait of this young girl? *(She was extremely talkative.)*

5) Why was Marilla going to force Anne to go back to the orphanage? *(She was not a boy, and that is what they requested.)*

6) What was Matthew's opinion on sending her back? *(He did not want to send her back; he was fascinated by her.)*

7) Why did Anne feel that it was not worth going outside to explore Green Gables? *(She would fall in love with it and then have to leave it.)*

8) Where was Marilla going to take Anne in order to send her back? *(Mrs. Spencer's house in White Sands)*

9) How did Anne's parents die? *(from the fever)*

10) Why did Mrs. Hammond and Mrs. Thomas take Anne in after she became an orphan? *(to help with their children)*

11) How did Mrs. Spencer suggest that they solve the problem of Anne? *(give her to Mrs. Blewett to help with their children)*

12) Why did Marilla not want to give Anne to Mrs. Blewett? *(Mrs. Blewett was a tough woman, stingy, and with a bad temper.)*

13) What did Anne think that God did on purpose, so she has never prayed to Him? *(gave her red hair)*

14) What did Anne thank God for? *(White Way of Delight, Lake of Shining Waters, Bonny and the Snow Queen)*

15) By what title did Anne want to call Marilla? *("Aunt" Marilla)*

16) What did Marilla require Anne to memorize in order to teach her to pray? *(The Lord's Prayer)*

17) How did Mrs. Rachel insult Anne? *(by saying she was skinny, homely, had lots of freckles and had "carrot" hair)*

18) How did Marilla support Anne to Mrs. Rachel? *(She told Mrs. Rachel that she shouldn't have teased Anne about her looks.)*

19) How was Anne encouraged to apologize to Mrs. Rachel? *(Matthew talked to her.)*

20) In what manner did Anne apologize to Mrs. Rachel? *(very dramatically with a lot of flowery language)*

2 Young people feel that it is okay to "talk back" or "blow up" when adults tease them or say something negative about them. Discuss with the class their opinions on whether or not Anne was right in her actions or if Mrs. Rachel was the one in the wrong. How could Anne have responded differently? What might Marilla have done to handle the situation better? What is the opinion of the "forced apology"? Were Anne's actions and apology acceptable? What should/could be done about them?

3 Although Mrs. Rachel should not have been so negative with Anne, the Bible says that we are to respect our elders and those in authority over us. Using the verses on **Master 5.1**, discuss how Mrs. Rachel should have talked to Anne or how Anne should have responded to Mrs. Rachel.

4 Plan a Pioneer Day. Encourage the students to dress up and to plan to teach younger students the customs and lifestyles of the early 1900's.

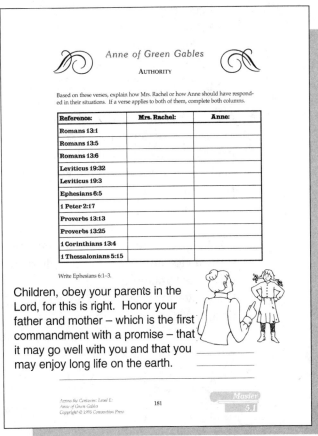

LESSON 6 CHAPTERS 11–12

Anne desperately wants a puffed-sleeve dress. Marilla thinks this is an unnecessary luxury. Anne's visit to church is boring, so she spends the time daydreaming about her puffed sleeves. When Anne reports on the church service, Marilla cannot help but secretly agree to some of the complaints. Although no one seems to care about Anne, Diana Barry finally comes home and becomes Anne's new friend.

1 Use any of the suggested activities to develop an understanding of the vocabulary listed for Chapters 11–20 on **Master I.1**. Assist students in making connections to previously learned information. For example, look for morphemes of similar meanings:

1) paragraph – sentences written together
   paraphrase – meanings restated together
2) fury / furious – anger
   infuriate – make angry
3) Beatitudes – Jesus' statements of blessing or happiness
   beatification – making someone happy

2 Assign the reading of Chapters 11–12. Follow the reading with discussion of the general events of the chapters. Continue to help students note the action-reaction sequences. Ask students whether the reactions should/could have been anticipated.
- Anne's dress doesn't have puffed sleeves.
- Anne wears flowers to church.
- Anne describes her church visit.
- Anne meets Diana.

3 Direct students to add Diana to the characterization section of their diaries. What type of person does she appear to be? Will Anne and Diana's friendship last? They appear to have very different personalities, so how do they complement each other?

4 After showing the students the typical clothing of young people during this time (**Master 6.1**), have them design their own ideal outfit. They should describe it in detail and provide an illustration or bring an example of it to share with the other students.

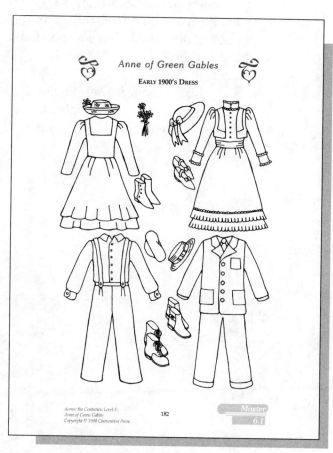

Across the Centuries: Level E:
Anne of Green Gables

LESSON 7   CHAPTERS 13–14

Anne comes home one day with exciting news. There is to be a Sunday school picnic. Marilla says that she may go and will even make a food basket for Anne. When Marilla's prized amethyst brooch disappears, Marilla insists that Anne took it. Anne continues to declare her innocence. Finally, Marilla states that Anne will not go to the picnic until she confesses. In desperation, Anne apologizes, but Marilla still refuses to let her go. Later Marilla finds the brooch. As her way of making up to Anne, she hurries to prepare a food basket so Anne may attend the picnic.

1 Ask students to share experiences in which they have been falsely accused. What happened? How did they feel? What did they do to try to resolve the problem? What happened after the accusation was proven false? As students read and discuss Chapters 13 and 14, encourage them to identify these feelings and reactions in Anne.

2 The students need to see the importance of having all of the facts before they accuse someone and to never assume something just because that is the initial hunch. Discuss how this could hurt someone and how often it will not be the true explanation. Secondly, discuss whether or not Anne should have confessed when she did not do anything wrong. How do the students feel about this lie of convenience? Lastly, Marilla's stubbornness caused a lot of the trouble. What kinds of problems does being stubborn cause? How could Marilla have handled things differently?

3 The Bible has many verses that refer to lying, and never is lying viewed as acceptable. Have the class look up the verses listed on **Master 7.1** and explain what each one says about lying. Is it ever justified?

4 Marilla says that she should have believed Anne because she had never known Anne to tell a lie. Why is it so important for you to keep your reputation pure and honest? Close this lesson by discussing this issue of lying. Ask students to list in their diaries arguments for and against the importance of keeping their reputation pure.

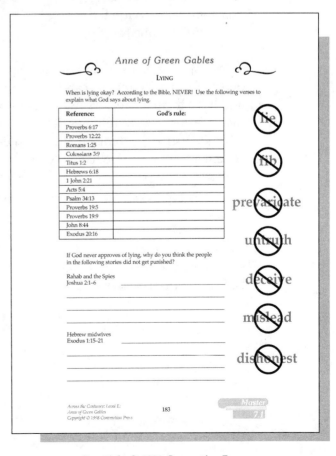

Across the Centuries: Level E: Anne of Green Gables

LESSON 8 CHAPTERS 15–16

School has begun. Diana is Anne's only bosom friend, but she gets along well with everyone else. The most popular boy in school, Gilbert Blythe, causes quite a stir on the first day. Not used to being ignored by girls, he is determined to make Anne notice him. Trying to get her attention, he calls Anne "Carrots." Anne immediately cracks her slate over his head. Gilbert tries to apologize, but nothing can mend Anne's hurt feelings. She tells Marilla that she is never going back to school, and Marilla allows her to stay home. One day Anne invites Diana to tea but accidentally serves a few glasses of currant wine instead of raspberry cordial. After Diana becomes drunk, Anne is forbidden by Mrs. Barry to associate with Diana anymore.

1 After reading the chapters, lead a class discussion of the events in Chapter 15. Once again Anne has to deal with her temper. Why do students think Gilbert says what he does? How should Anne have taken the insult? Who is wrong in the situation? Does the teacher make it worse, or is he trying to make it better? Does Marilla make the right decision in allowing Anne to stay home? What would you have done if Anne was your child? Discuss the incident with Diana. What will be the result of this problem?

2 The scene between Gilbert and Anne is a very dramatic one and lends itself to being acted out. Divide the class into groups of four or five and have them discuss how they want to act it out. Give them 10 to 15 minutes it to plan their scene. You could also divide the chapter so that every group is working on a different scene. Allow time for groups to present their re-enactments.

3 Who is really at fault in this new feud between Gilbert and Anne? In debate format, divide the class into two teams. Assign each group one character and have them list reasons which support their character's innocence in the argument. After 10 to 15 minutes, let them debate the other group. Each group should have an opening statement, at least three different supporting points and a closing statement. When these have been stated, open the floor for questions and arguments. Assign points for each statement, supporting point, question and argument; then announce which team has accumulated the most points.

4 Place the items below on cards and distribute them to pairs of students. Discuss the concept of: Responsible for My Response. Let pairs discuss, then share with the class, an example from the book and a personal life lesson that can be learned from each example.

Responsible for My Response

Being openly embarrassed or criticized in front of others	Unintentionally causing harm to another person	Being too hasty to jump to conclusions
Not getting something you really wanted	Being teased about something very sensitive to you	Being separated from a good friend
Being falsely accused	Being bored	Being misunderstood by others
Telling a lie of convenience	Speaking without thinking	Wanting so badly to please someone, but failing

5 Assign the following questions as a writing exercise in students' diaries: If Anne was your child, would you let her stay home because of the argument with Gilbert? What would you have done? Students should also begin a page in their diaries for the characterization of Gilbert.

LESSON 9 CHAPTERS 17–18

Anne decides to return to school. All of the girls are really nice to her, and at school she can see Diana. Gilbert and Anne compete for first place in the class. While Marilla is away, Anne is summoned by a distraught Diana to help save her little sister who has become very sick with the croup. Anne knows exactly what to do. When Mrs. Barry gets home, the doctor tells her that Anne saved the little girl's life. Mrs. Barry apologizes to Anne. The two girls are now allowed to be friends again.

1 This section of the book marks a change in people's perceptions of Anne. Place a chart labeled "Before" and "After" before students and let them suggest characteristics of Anne to this point (*impulsive, poor judgment, immature, etc.*). Explain that a major shift in perspective is often related to a crisis event. For example, a person thought to be monstrous saves the life of a child. People then realize that he is gentle and kind. Encourage students to watch for this transition. (The "After" section of your chart can be completed throughout the remaining lessons as more positive traits are encountered.)

2 After reading the chapters, discuss these questions: When Anne is not allowed to be friends with Diana, what project does she devote herself to? What do the students think will happen between Anne and Gilbert? Why is Anne trying so hard to ignore Gilbert? Discuss the events which surround Anne and Diana becoming friends again. What if Mrs. Barry still hadn't forgiven Anne; how should Anne respond?

3 Encourage students to research information about Canada's government. Do they have elected officials? Are there political parties similar to America? Assign mini-reports to volunteers to present to the class.

4 Have volunteers prepare a newscast which covers both the Canadian Premier's visit and the "local news" of Anne saving Minnie Mae. Divide the class into groups and let them prepare a ten minute newscast to be videotaped and watched later. They can include the news, weather, entertainment, sports and items of human interest.

5 Have students use their diaries to react to the following questions. When Anne and Diana say goodbye, they exchange a lock of hair. What are some ways today that friends pledge their allegiance to each other? Have you tried any of them?

LESSON 10 — CHAPTERS 19–20

For Diana's birthday, she has invited Anne to a local concert. When they return, the girls race to the bed but end up jumping on Diana's elderly Aunt Josephine. The lady is outraged. Anne apologizes and becomes friends with Aunt Josephine. Anne's imagination gets out of control while pretending there are ghosts in the woods. She becomes terrified to walk to Diana's house after dark.

1 Discuss with students how the title of Chapter 19 foreshadows what will happen. Before reading the chapter, what do they think the catastrophe will be? Assign the reading of the chapters.

2 Discuss the following questions as students react to the chapter. Characterize Aunt Josephine. What is she really like? Why are she and Anne "kindred spirits"? Why do the Barrys not get along with Aunt Josephine like Anne does? Discuss Anne's imagination again. Has it finally gone too far? Can an imagination ever go too far? What are some examples to support your answer? Let the students share times when they have been scared by their own imaginations.

3 At the Debating Club concert, there was a collection of stories, songs and poems presented. Prepare a list of classic poems and songs from which the students can choose to memorize. They can present them on a specific date to parents and the class.

4 Discuss the difference between fantasy and reality with the class. In *Anne of Green Gables*, there are numerous examples of both. Using **Master 10.1**, have students identify five examples of each from the book and five examples that could be both. Discuss their choices.

5 The students are now at the approximate mid-point of the book. Allow time for some general review, especially of Chapters 11–20.

1) Why was Anne disappointed in the dresses Marilla made for her? *(They were plain and did not have puffed sleeves.)*

2) Why was Anne not interested in Mr. Bell's prayer? *(It was long, boring and not directed toward her.)*

3) Whom did Anne want as her bosom friend? *(Diana Barry)*

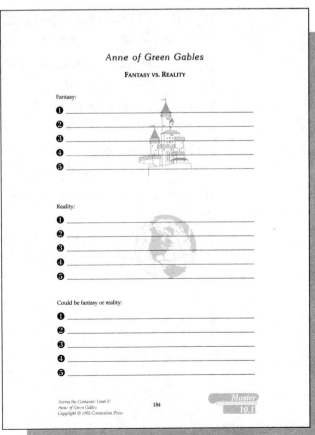

Across the Centuries: Level E:
Anne of Green Gables

157

Copyright © 1998 Convention Press

4) What did Anne and Diana promise to each other? *(to be faithful friends forever and ever)*

5) What kind of event happened that Anne had never experienced before? *(a Sunday School picnic)*

6) Why was Marilla's amethyst brooch so important to her? *(It was a family heirloom and had a braid of her mother's hair in it.)*

7) Where did Anne say that she lost Marilla's brooch? *(She dropped it in the Lake of Shining Waters.)*

8) Why did Anne feel the need to apologize? *(so she could be allowed to go to the picnic)*

9) How did Gilbert Blythe try to get Anne's attention? *(picked up a piece of her braid and called her "Carrots")*

10) After lunch, what ultimate insult did the teacher give Anne and Gilbert? *(He made Anne sit beside Gilbert.)*

11) What happened to Diana when she went to tea at Anne's house? *(Diana got drunk on currant wine.)*

12) What did Mrs. Barry say the punishment for these actions was to be? *(Diana was no longer allowed to be friends with Anne.)*

13) Why did Anne go back to school after she was no longer allowed to see Diana? *(She needed something else to concentrate on.)*

14) Who was Anne's biggest rival at school? *(Gilbert Blythe)*

15) Why did Diana come and ask Anne for help when Minnie Mae was sick? *(All the adults were in town.)*

16) Why did Anne know what to do for Minnie Mae's croup? *(She had looked after other young children.)*

17) How did Diana celebrate her birthday? *(by going to the Debating Club concert and having Anne spend the night in the spare bedroom)*

18) How did the evening end in disaster because of the spare bedroom? *(Aunt Josephine had come to spend the night, and they jumped on her in the bed.)*

19) Why did Aunt Josephine finally relent from her anger? *(Anne apologized and charmed her.)*

20) Why was Anne afraid to go through the woods at night? *(She and Diana had created stories about it being haunted, and she started believing them.)*

LESSON 11 CHAPTERS 21–22

At the beginning of summer, the teacher and the local pastor are replaced. The new pastor's family is invited to Green Gables for tea. Although Anne's cake is a disaster, she discovers a good friend in Mrs. Allan. Anne also hears news about the new teacher, Miss Stacy. Anne anxiously awaits the new school year.

1 Direct students to their vocabulary lists on **Master I.1**. Assign one word to each student to research and explain to the class. As appropriate, they should illustrate and provide examples of the word's use.

2 As a pre-set exercise, let students share experiences in which they really wanted to impress someone but created a big embarrassment through a foolish mistake. Assign the reading of Chapters 21 and 22, then discuss the general sequence of events. Do they sympathize with Anne's feelings? What could they say to encourage Anne?

3 Have the students write a character sketch of Mrs. Allan in their diaries. What is there about the new pastor's wife that would be attractive to Anne? Is this the type of person that Anne wants to be?

4 Challenge students to think about the person they would like to become. Direct students to think about the traits of one or two older persons they really admire— perhaps a family member, teacher or friend. They can make a list of the traits most desired in their own lives as they grow older. Duplicate **Master 11.1** on colorful paper and let students copy their lists. Post the lists on a bulletin board entitled: The Person I Want to Become.

5 Use student diaries to react to the following scenario: Anne is extremely excited to be invited to tea with Mrs. Allan. What is something that you would like to be invited to? Why?

LESSON 12   CHAPTERS 23–24

At Diana's party, Josie dares Anne to walk the ridgepole on the Barry's roof. Anne takes the dare. She makes it several feet before losing her balance and falling. Confined to bed for several weeks because of the injury, Anne misses the beginning of school. When she returns to school, she realizes what a wonderful teacher Miss Stacy really is. When Miss Stacy plans a Christmas concert, Anne excitedly joins in the preparations.

1 After reading the chapters, lead the class in the following discussion items. Many times young people do things they are dared to do because it seems to make them popular or, at least, fit in. Although Anne is not overly concerned with fitting in, her honor is at stake, so she foolishly takes the dare. Discuss with the students what she could have done differently in the situation. What would they have done? Take a poll of how many students would have taken the dare. What are students often dared to do today? Why is it hard to say "No"?

2 Using their diaries, direct students to complete a character analysis of Miss Stacy. Discuss what makes a good teacher.

3 As a class, brainstorm the rewriting of Chapter 23 so that Anne says "No" to the dare. What other potential directions could occur in the plot? How could the ending change?

4 Let students develop and conduct a confidential survey as to the types of dares students will try. Consider the following questions: What types of dares? Why did they try it? What do they think will happen if they don't take the dare? What is accomplished in accepting a dare? What harms could result?

5 Using the student diaries, have the class list the qualities of a great student in comparison to those of a great teacher.

LESSON 13   CHAPTERS 25–26

It's Christmas and Matthew undertakes the task of buying Anne a fashionable dress with puffed sleeves. After embarrassing himself at the local store, he finally asks Mrs. Rachel's help. Anne is thrilled with the new dress and wears it to the school concert. Matthew and Marilla discuss the need to start saving for a higher education for Anne. A creative writing club becomes an important part of Anne's life.

1 Place another chart labeled "Before" and "After" next to the one students are completing for Anne. Assign this one to Matthew. Let students suggest characteristics for him (*quiet, peacemaker, lets Marilla have her way, loves Anne, etc.*). Explain that characteristics (and our perceptions of them) not only change because of a crisis, but can change over time due to a growing belief in what's right. Encourage students to note this transition in Matthew as they read the next chapters.

2 Review vocabulary and assign Chapters 25 and 26. After the reading, direct the discussion of the significant events.

3 It is important to study Matthew's character development in Chapter 25. He has been viewed previously as a quiet man who enjoys having Anne around, but not too much is said about him. However, in this chapter we see the real Matthew. Discuss how unselfish, loving, thoughtful and strong Matthew is as he purchases one of Anne's fondest wishes. Focus on the talk that Matthew and Marilla have concerning Anne's future. Direct students to extend the descriptions of Matthew in the characterization section of their diaries.

4 Matthew and Marilla desire Anne to become a teacher, a job often held by young women in the early 1900's. Ask if any students would like to become teachers at age 16. Why or why not? What challenges would they face?

5 Giving surprise gifts is not something that most young people do today. Divide the class into groups of three or four. Have each group choose a person in the school that they would like to surprise with a gift. Then have them plan how they are going to surprise this person. Make sure they choose something that will be appreciated and special to the person—not just something to fulfill the assignment.

6 Anne and her friends write enough stories to fill a book. Encourage the class to do the same. Assign a creative writing project. Encourage poetry, fiction and nonfiction. Involve student artists to illustrate the book, and then collect all the writings. Have student editors publish the book. Give a copy to every student.

7 According to Anne, she is trying to watch how she speaks about others because, "Mrs. Allan says we should never make uncharitable speeches." Use **Master 13.1** as a guide for discussing what the Bible says about a Christian's speech and how we should respond to those around us.

8 Use student diaries to write reactions to these questions: Knowing Marilla's personality and what she thinks is important, why do you think she has never made Anne a pretty dress? Why does Matthew think she has never done it? Is it right or wrong, or is it just a matter of opinion?

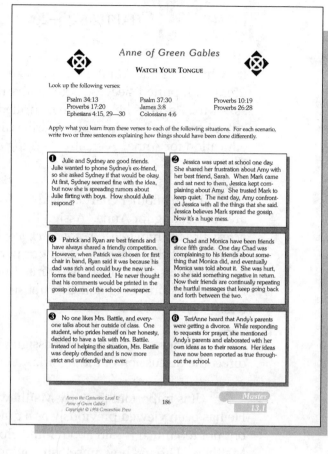

LESSON 14   CHAPTERS 27–28

One evening Anne is nowhere to be found. Anne has mistakenly dyed her hair green. When she returns home, she hides in her room. As a last resort, Marilla must cut Anne's hair extremely short. Later Anne role-plays a death scene. She climbs into a small boat, pretends to be dead and begins to float down the river. The boat begins to sink. Her rescuer is Gilbert Blythe. Before they part, Gilbert apologizes for past insults but is rebuffed by Anne's lack of forgiveness.

1 Assign small groups of students to share in reading aloud Chapters 27 and 28. They can discuss Anne's antics as they enjoy the reading. Assign the task of identifying two areas in which they can most identify with Anne's emotions and continuing problems. List and discuss these after the groups finish the chapters.

2 Pride is the theme of the chapters. Anne dyes her hair in order to be more attractive and scorns a genuine apology by Gilbert. Discuss with students how difficult it was for Anne to admit she was wrong. Ask how they might have responded in each situation. Would they really have acted differently? How should Anne have acted, especially with Gilbert? Read and discuss Proverbs 28:13 in relation to Anne's actions.

3 All of us face embarrassing moments when we are young, and it is often difficult to know how to act. Using the scenarios on **Master 14.1**, have the students discuss how they might act in each situation.

4 Anne and her friends are fascinated by the Camelot era. Bring a video about King Arthur and the Knights of the Round Table. Have students research the main characters (King Arthur, Guinevere and Lancelot) from this time period and present a report on them. Devote a bulletin board to this time period with pictures, articles and reports.

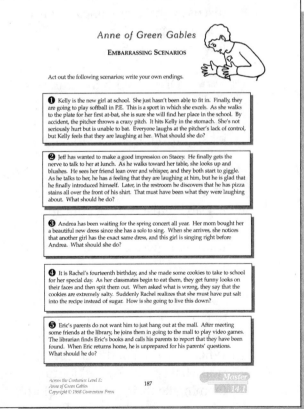

5 Read the poem by Tennison as a class. As a project at home and in groups, have the students act out this poem and videotape it. Have them bring their videos to show the class.

6 Have the students use their diaries to react to the following question: When Anne dyes her hair, she is trying to satisfy her vanity. What have you done in order to make yourself look better that has ended in disaster and taught you a valuable lesson?

Across the Centuries: Level E: 163   Copyright © 1998 Convention Press
Anne of Green Gables

LESSON 15 CHAPTERS 29–30

Aunt Josephine has invited Diana and Anne to stay with her and attend the Exhibition. They see numerous booths and exhibits and even a horse race. Aunt Josephine takes the girls to an opera. After returning home, Marilla has surprising news for Anne. Miss Stacy wants Anne to join a class for students interested in going to Queen's for teacher training. Anne eagerly joins the class and works harder than ever to prove herself in comparison to Gilbert. At the same time, Anne is worried about Matthew's health.

1 Return to the "Before and After" chart that describes Anne's changing characteristics. Let students suggest additional terms to add to the chart. (Likely, the negatives will outweigh the positives.) Explain that significant changes are about to occur and that students should look for precipitating events and Anne's reactions. Assign the reading of Chapters 29 and 30.

2 After students complete the assigned reading, let them discuss the changes they see in Anne and suggest descriptions for the "After" section of the chart. The students can continue to expand their characterization of Anne in their diaries. In one chapter, Anne seems to grow from a young girl into a young woman. As you discuss ways that Anne has grown up, encourage students that they will also reach maturity and will face many life choices. In the early 1900's, women only had a few choices in professional occupations—one being a teacher.

3 Discuss with the students what they would like to be when they are older. Why are they choosing these particular jobs? Encourage them to have the dedication that is needed to succeed in these areas. Given a list of occupations (**Master 15.1**), have the students work in groups to research what type of education is required in each job, what other types of training is necessary, and what skills are involved.

4 An Exhibition is similar to a county fair. Using graph paper, let the students prepare a layout of a fairground. Where are each of the exhibits (animals, rides, baked goods, etc.) located? Let them make their graphs as colorful and creative as possible, then display them on a bulletin board.

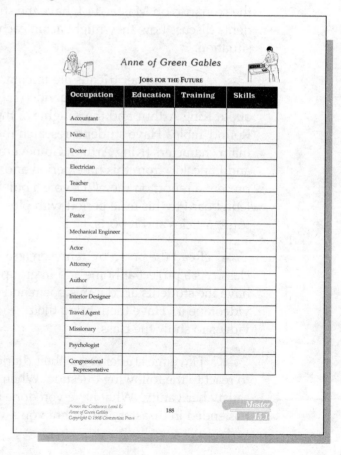

Across the Centuries: Level E: Anne of Green Gables

5 As we grow up, there are a lot of things that change, even if we don't want them to. Encourage students to discuss the following questions in small groups: Think of the next five years of your life. What will change, both inwardly and outwardly? What will stay the same? What will change that you may not want? What changes are you most anticipating?

6 Review the progression of the story to date. Especially focus on students' knowledge of Chapters 21 through 30.

1) What was Anne's opinion about the new pastor and his wife? *(She was very impressed with them and wanted to especially impress Mrs. Allan.)*

2) How did Anne mess up the cake when she tried to impress Mrs. Alan? *(She used anodyne liniment instead of vanilla.)*

3) Why did Marilla think that Anne need not get too excited about her invitation to tea with Mrs. Allan? *(Mrs. Allan had promised to invite all the young girls to tea.)*

4) Why was Mrs. Lynde worried about the new teacher that had been hired? *(She was a woman.)*

5) Why was Anne so adamant that she had to walk the ridgepole? *(Her honor was at stake.)*

6) What was most upsetting to Anne about breaking her ankle? *(She wouldn't be at school to meet the new teacher.)*

7) What was unique about Miss Stacy's teaching style? *(She let the children learn a lot on their own by taking them on field trips, playing games and letting them do their own research.)*

8) What event was Miss Stacy arranging that would be the first of its kind at the small school? *(a concert)*

9) Why did Matthew feel that Anne needed a new dress with puffed sleeves? *(She always had plain dresses, and she looked different from the other girls.)*

10) Whom did Matthew ask to help him with Anne's new dress? *(Mrs. Rachel Lynde)*

11) Why did Anne and her friends form the Story Club? *(to encourage their creativity for the stories Miss Stacy assigned)*

12) Why did Anne feel that there was some hope that she could be like Mrs. Allan when she grew up? *(Mrs. Allan also got into a lot of trouble as a child.)*

13) What color was Anne trying to dye her hair when it turned green? *(black)*

14) What was the only way Anne could repair her hair? *(cut it all off)*

15) How did Anne end up being the one who played the role of Elaine? *(The others were too scared.)*

16) What did Gilbert say he would never do again after Anne rejected him for the second time? *(ask for her forgiveness)*

17) Who invited Anne and Diana to go to the Exhibition in Charlottetown? *(Aunt Josephine)*

18) How did Anne feel about being rich every day? *(It leaves no room for imagination.)*

19) Why did Anne think that Miss Stacy had come to visit Marilla? *(She had gotten in trouble for reading* Ben Hur.*)*

20) When would the extra preparation for the Queen's exam be held? *(after school every day for a few hours)*

LESSON 16 CHAPTERS 31–32

Anne has nightmares that she will fail her exam. Marilla and Matthew both know Anne will leave them one day. At the end of the school year, Miss Stacy announces that she will not return. The students must travel to Charlottetown and spend two grueling days in examinations. Gilbert and Anne pass with the highest marks and tie for first place.

1 Refer to **Master I.1** and the final list of vocabulary terms. Read the following sentences and ask students to identify a related word in their list. Challenge them to restate the sentence (or state another one) using the word from their list.

1) The <u>instant</u> oatmeal was ready in less than a minute.

2) Mark proved himself most <u>able</u> and <u>capable</u> of winning.

3) The boys who set off the fireworks created a <u>scandal</u>.

4) Pay attention and obey my every <u>beck</u> and call.

5) What was life like in the <u>Province</u> of Nova Scotia?

6) When you get a leg cramp, rub the muscles <u>vigorously</u>.

7) What kind of <u>grub</u> do you like to eat on camping trips?

8) Mom said it was just <u>wishful</u> thinking.

9) <u>Sentimental</u> thoughts carried her heart back to childhood days.

10) Mr. Graham is a person of importance to be <u>noticed</u> and respected.

11) He carried a bouquet of <u>narcissus</u> and grieved in loneliness following her rejection.

12) Stop! All unauthorized persons are <u>prohibited</u> from entering the area.

13) Stacy Ames won the Miss <u>Congeniality</u> title for her friendliness during the beauty pageant.

14) Pastor James taught us that true love never <u>ceases</u> or fails; it continues forever.

15) Little Aaron sucked his thumb, pouted and <u>sulked</u> all day.

16) The goal seemed distant and <u>intangible</u>, not attainable regardless of our efforts.

17) The <u>tenants</u> of the first-floor apartments needed to <u>attend</u> the residents' meeting with the <u>superintendent</u>.

18) The butterflies gaily danced as they <u>fluttered</u> from blossom to blossom.

19) Being 6'4" and 300 pounds of bone and muscle, Mr. Beck's <u>stoutness</u> easily intimidated the young boys.

20) It's not unusual for a grieving person to <u>languish</u> in sorrow and self-pity.

2 After reading Chapters 31 and 32, lead the class in a discussion of the events and Anne's responses. Especially focus on her concerns for taking the examination. Anne is like most students when it comes to taking tests. She is never secure in what she knows. Discuss with the class what is difficult for them about taking tests. What are the best kind of tests? What situations are most stressful? Let the students share examples of how they deal with stress. What are some examples of times when students have worried about something that they should not have worried about because everything turned out okay?

3 Have your students complete a chart on "Anne: Then and Now" (**Master 16.1**). How is she maturing? How has she changed? Students may refer to your class chart as needed.

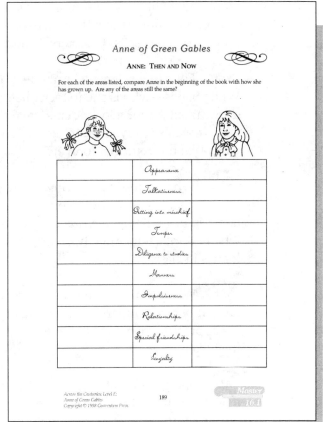

4 As an art project, have the students bring magazines, crayons, markers and glue. The focus of this project is "success." Have them design a collage with their ideas. They can use words, pictures and slogans. Display the collages when they are finished.

5 Students in this age group often focus on what they would like to do with their lives. Take a survey of what the students would like to be. Choose three to five of the more popular choices and invite someone from these areas to talk to the students.

LESSON 17 CHAPTERS 33–34

Anne has always dreamed of reciting a work at a concert. She is invited to recite before the Avonlea community. A professional speaker recites before Anne. When she is called to the stage, Gilbert Blythe looks right at her and smiles. Sensing his encouragement, she captivates her audience with her original recitation and her encore. Anne arrives at Queen's to continue her education. Both she and Gilbert decide to try the advanced courses. She feels more secure with Gilbert in her classes.

1 Review vocabulary. Ask students to share experiences in which two people who "fought like cats and dogs" when they were younger, grew up to be friends. Encourage students to note the changing relationship between Anne and Gilbert as they read and discuss Chapters 33 and 34.

2 For a few moments, Anne feels out of place when she is at the concert in White Sands—who is she to recite before these important people? What does this show about Anne? Do students have similar experiences? Discuss the fact that Gilbert seems to give her strength as she recites, even though she doesn't see it that way. Will this feud last forever?

3 When Anne is preparing to say goodbye to Matthew and Marilla, Marilla does not quite know how to put her feelings into words. She rather envies Anne's talent in never being at a loss for words. Encourage students to prepare a dialogue where Marilla tells Anne how she feels about her. Let students perform the dialogues in class.

4 When Anne is homesick at Queen's, she starts thinking about everyone she has left behind. Too many times we do not take the time to tell others how much we appreciate them. Have the students write a letter of appreciation to anyone they like. After editing the letters, provide assistance in mailing them.

5 Assign students to write a reaction essay in their diaries. Since coming to live at Green Gables, friends have been very important to Anne. Why are friends important to you? How do you support and encourage your friends? How do they do the same for you?

LESSON 18 — CHAPTERS 35–36

The year at Queen's is almost over. The final exams once again have the students worried. Anne is extremely jealous of Gilbert's attention to Ruby Gillis. However, she convinces herself that she is not interested. Her goal is to win the medal and the Avery scholarship. The results of the examinations are posted. Anne wins the Avery scholarship. Gilbert wins the medal. They have tied. After Anne returns home, Matthew's health continues to worsen. Anne comments that she sometimes wishes she had been a boy so that she could be more helpful to Matthew.

1 After students read and discuss Chapters 35 and 36, help them focus on the foreshadowing that hints how the book will end. First, Anne is jealous of Gilbert's friendships with other girls. This will need to be resolved before the book ends. Second, Anne cannot imagine going to college without Gilbert being there. How could this problem be solved? Last, Matthew's health is a main issue in this section. He is not getting better. What might happen to him before the end of the book? Discuss with the students these examples of foreshadowing and let them make predictions about what will happen.

2 In relation to the discussions on foreshadowing, have the students write the last chapter. What will happen? They need to write at least two to three pages in order to tie all of the events together.

3 Hold class outside for a day. Maintain a comfortable workload, but let the students enjoy the time spent outdoors. Relate the experience of Anne's returning from Queen's.

4 Use the following for a class debate: Mrs. Rachel does not believe that women should be educated higher than high school. This was a very popular opinion during this time. Pretend that you live in the early 1900's, on which side of the issue would you be? Why?

Lesson 19 Chapters 37–38

Matthew passes away while holding a letter stating that the Abbey Bank has failed. The entire community mourns Matthew's death. For a while Anne feels guilty for laughing again, but she realizes that Matthew liked it best when she was laughing. Later Marilla goes to the eye doctor and finds that she is going blind. Marilla decides to sell Green Gables and Anne decides to give up her scholarship and teach in Carmody. Gilbert assigns Anne to the Avonlea school so that she can remain at home. Anne is overwhelmed and finally approaches Gilbert to thank him. He is excited to think that they can now be friends.

1 Remind students of the foreshadowing of Matthew's death. Explain that in the book (just as in life), some problems are inconsequential or fixable; others are not. *(Hair turned green was cut off; a broken ankle healed; Anne was rescued from the river.)* Death is not fixable; it must be accepted and life must go on. As they read and discuss Chapters 37 and 38, challenge students to look for these life-changing problems and how the characters respond to them.

2 When Matthew dies, it is amazing how many people come to honor him at the funeral. What made everyone like him? How was he able to affect that many lives when he was so quiet and unassuming? What character traits did he show that other people appreciated? Read Isaiah 32:17; 1 Thessalonians 4:11–12 and Proverbs 22:1. Discuss how the verses characterize Matthew's life. You may want to use **Master 19.1** for students to write an epitaph, poem or summary to honor Matthew.

3 While the book conveys Christian principles, it does not specifically address a Biblical view of death. Read 1 Thessalonians 4:13–18; then 1 Corinthians 15:42–44 and 51–52; then 2 Corinthians 54:14–18. Lead students in a discussion of a Christian's perspective on death. For example:

- We are sad but know we have hope in eternal life.
- To be absent from the body is to be present with the Lord.
- Everyone eventually dies. Therefore, eternity is more important than time on earth.

4 Discuss the two examples of sacrifice. Anne is willing to postpone her education in order to be with Marilla and to save Green Gables. Gilbert gives up the Avonlea school for Anne. What do these sacrifices mean to each relationship? How are they examples of the way Christians should treat each other?

5 Review the last section of the book by focusing on the general sequence of events, as well as specific information for Chapters 31–38.

1) What was the doctor's advice about Anne's summer vacation? *(that she spend as much time as possible outside)*

2) What did Marilla notice as the biggest change in Anne that summer? *(She did not talk as much.)*

3) For Anne, what subject had the worst examination? *(geometry)*

4) How well did Anne and Gilbert pass the exam? *(They tied for first place.)*

5) What was Anne's goal for when she recited at the White Sands concert? *(to make the audience cry)*

6) When Anne was about to give in to stage freight, what kept her going? *(the thought of Gilbert laughing at her)*

7) What three things did Anne say made her rich? *(being sixteen, being happy as a queen, and having an imagination)*

8) Why did Marilla say that she wished she had Anne's flair for words? *(so she could tell Anne how much she meant to her)*

9) The Avery Scholarship was an award for what subject? *(English)*

10) Who was Gilbert dating while at Queen's? *(Ruby Gillis)*

11) Why did Aunt Josephine like the fact that Anne was so lovable? *(because she didn't have to try to love her)*

12) Who won the Queen's medal? *(Gilbert)* Who won the Avery scholarship? *(Anne)*

13) What was Anne planning to do in the fall now that she had won the Avery? *(go to Redmond for college)*

14) Why did the doctor say that Matthew died from shock? *(He got a letter about the bank closing.)*

15) Whom did Anne turn to as she worked through her grief? *(Marilla)*

16) Why did Dr. Spencer say that Marilla had to see a specialist? *(Her eyes were hurting.)*

17) What did the specialist say about Marilla's eyes? *(She was going blind and must give up all strenuous activities.)*

18) How did Anne help keep Marilla from selling Green Gables? *(She decided to stay home and teach.)*

19) Who told Anne that Gilbert had given the Avonlea school to Anne? *(Mrs. Rachel Lynde)*

20) Why did Anne say that she spent half an hour talking to Gilbert at the gate? *(They had five years of lost conversations to catch up with.)*

6 As a method of review, list the main individuals students encountered and direct them to choose one incident that best characterizes the person they chose. They can share their choices in small groups.

7 Discuss as a class the developing plot of the story, the themes, and how the author wove the incidents together to show the changes in each person's character. Review the book by assigning various sections for student teams to write and role-play the dialogues.

- Marilla and Matthew decide whether or not to keep Anne.
- Mrs. Rachel Lynde meets Anne for the first time.
- Anne is accused of stealing the brooch.
- Anne and Diana have a tea party.
- Gilbert teases Anne about her red hair.
- Anne saves the life of Diana's little sister.
- Anne walks the ridgepole.
- Matthew buys a fashionable dress for Anne.
- Anne dyes her hair.
- Anne and Gilbert pass the test and attend Queen's.
- Matthew dies.
- Gilbert walks Anne home and they talk.

8 Provide an evaluation of the skills and information students have learned in the unit.

1) Use **Master 19.2a** and **b** as a unit test.

2) Choose and modify questions suggested throughout the unit to develop a test more complementary to your instructional goals.

3) Evaluate students' diaries and/or one or more of the summary activities.

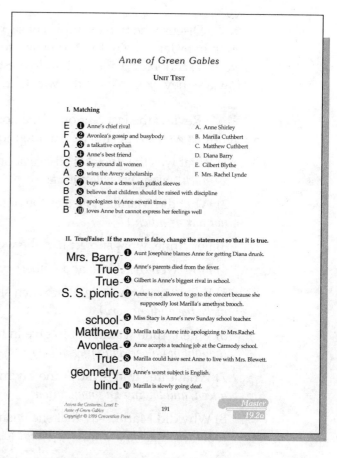

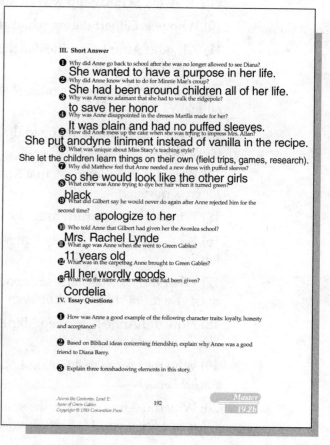

Across the Centuries: Level E:
Anne of Green Gables

ENRICHMENT

1 There are numerous concerts and plays which Anne attends. Take a field trip to a variety show, concert or play and compare it with the ones which Anne attended.

2 *Anne of Green Gables* is one of the most popular book sites on the World Wide Web. If you have access to the Internet, spend a class period browsing the Web pages related to *Anne of Green Gables*, Prince Edward Island or L. M. Montgomery.

3 There is an excellent movie of *Anne of Green Gables* and its sequel, *Anne of Avonlea*. When you complete the book, plan for the students to see the movie. Compare/contrast the movie with the book.

4 If some of the students have difficulty with reading comprehension, this book is on audiotape. It might be beneficial to use it as a listening exercise.

5 Challenge student authors with this assignment: Anne was always getting herself into trouble. Based on what you know about Anne, her friends, and her community, write your own Anne-type adventure story.

6 What is another mess in which Anne could have become involved? Act it out and videotape it.

7 Although orphanages do not exist like they used to, there are still plenty of group homes for children. Check into having the class volunteer at one of these locations for a day. Plan to take snacks and play games with the children.

8 Anne attends an opera for the first time in her life. To share her experience, bring a video or an audio recording of opera music. Discuss the characteristics of opera music with students. Ask them to outline the chapters as the music is played.

9 Have students write an essay in their diaries about losing someone special. When we lose someone special, it is often hard to start living again as though everything was normal. How do you think you could make it through the rough times?

10 Let the students brainstorm about what could happen in the next book as they think about the story line. What would they like to see happen?

Anne of Green Gables

VOCABULARY LIST

Chapters 1–10

1. traverse
2. gauntlet
3. scant
4. profound
5. sidle
6. quench
7. tempestuous
8. perturb
9. aloft
10. reverie
11. homely
12. sorrel
13. reproach
14. grim
15. regal
16. disposition
17. vexed
18. gravitate
19. benefactor
20. meditate

Chapters 11–20

1. furbelows
2. paraphrase
3. tremulous
4. infuriate
5. brooch
6. confound
7. beatification
8. lissome
9. indignant
10. rakish
11. contempt
12. torrent
13. coax
14. ostentatious
15. wistful
16. croup
17. oblivion
18. pompadour
19. prim
20. tapestry

Chapters 21–30

1. dunce
2. frank
3. mortify
4. kindle
5. ridgepole
6. kindred
7. laudable
8. suppress
9. trifle
10. tolerant
11. humdrum
12. turbulent
13. untimely
14. quiver
15. provident
16. placid
17. gable
18. hearth
19. impulsive
20. scruple

Chapters 31–38

1. scandalous
2. beckon
3. flutter
4. grubbing
5. incapable
6. notable
7. stout
8. languid
9. tenant
10. provincial
11. sentiment
12. vigor
13. narcissus
14. instantaneous
15. wistful
16. sulk
17. prohibit
18. tangible
19. unceasing
20. congenial

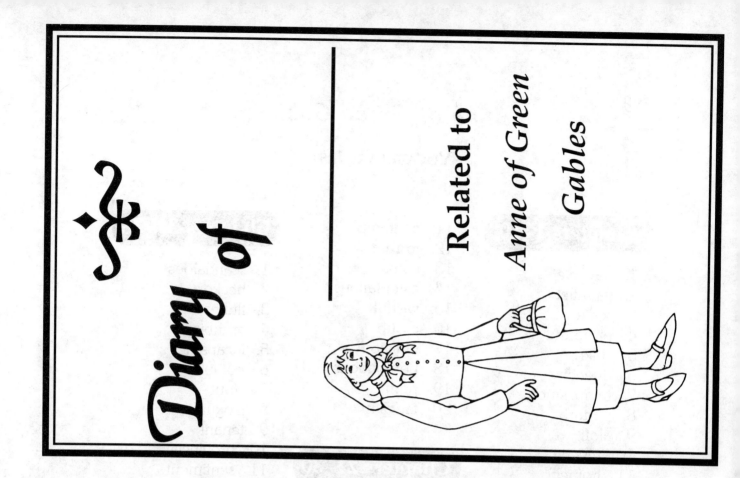

Diary of _____

Related to *Anne of Green Gables*

Some Life Lessons from *Anne of Green Gables*:

1. _____
2. _____
3. _____
4. _____
5. _____

Date

Entry

Date

Entry

Across the Centuries: Level E:
Anne of Green Gables
Copyright © 1998 Convention Press

Anne of Green Gables
THE GIFT OF SALVATION

Reference:	Gift:	Our Response:
Acts 4:12		
Acts 28:28		
Romans 1:16		
2 Corinthians 1:6		
Jonah 2:9		
1 Thessalonians 5:9		
2 Timothy 3:15		
Hebrews 2:3		
1 Peter 1:5		
2 Peter 3:15		
Revelation 19:1		

Anne of Green Gables

THE LORD'S PRAYER

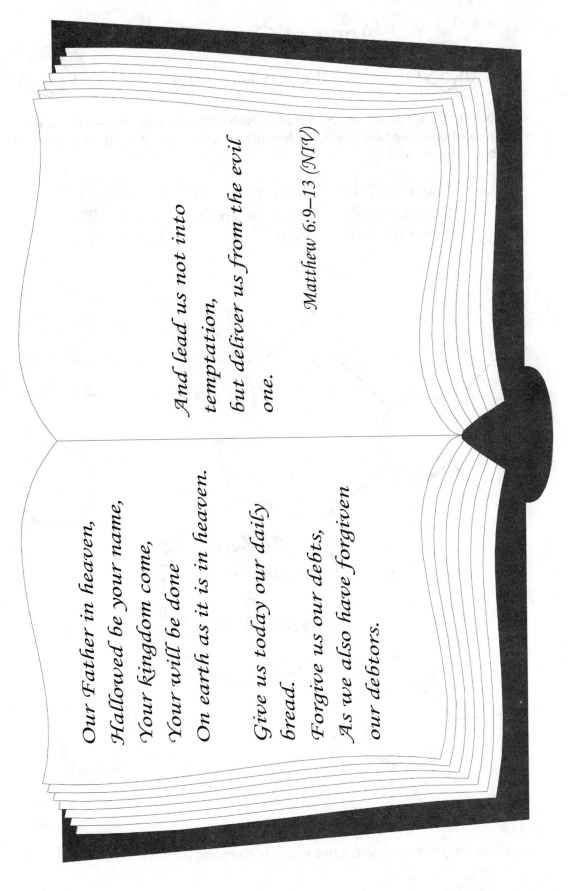

Our Father in heaven,
Hallowed be your name,
Your kingdom come,
Your will be done
On earth as it is in heaven.
Give us today our daily bread.
Forgive us our debts,
As we also have forgiven our debtors.
And lead us not into temptation,
but deliver us from the evil one.

Matthew 6:9–13 (NIV)

Across the Centuries: Level E:
Anne of Green Gables
Copyright © 1998 Convention Press

Master 4.1

Anne of Green Gables

BIBLICAL FRIENDSHIP

Look up the following verses. What do each of the commandments or stories reveal about what God wants our friendships to be like? What do they teach us about true friends?

Proverbs 17:17	Proverbs 27:10	John 15:14
Proverbs 18:24	Proverbs 16:28	James 2:23
Proverbs 27:6	John 15:13	James 4:4

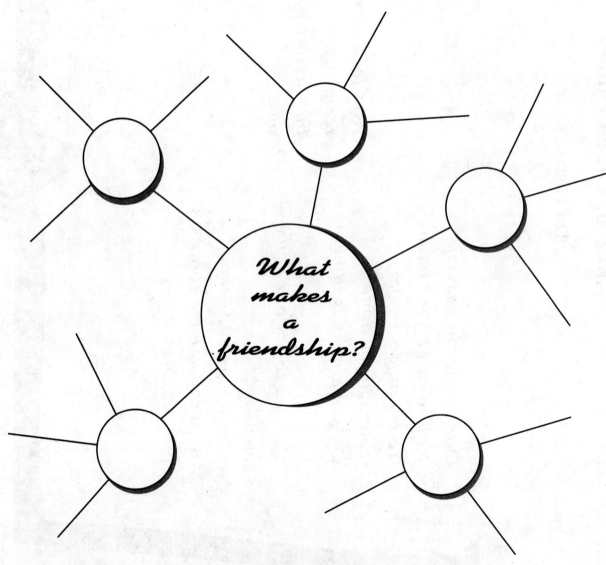

Fill in categories and descriptive words to complete the web.

Across the Centuries: Level E:
Anne of Green Gables
Copyright © 1998 Convention Press

Anne of Green Gables

AUTHORITY

Based on these verses, explain how Mrs. Rachel or how Anne should have responded in their situations. If a verse applies to both of them, complete both columns.

Reference:	Mrs. Rachel:	Anne:
Romans 13:1		
Romans 13:5		
Romans 13:6		
Leviticus 19:32		
Leviticus 19:3		
Ephesians 6:5		
1 Peter 2:17		
Proverbs 13:13		
Proverbs 13:25		
1 Corinthians 13:4		
1 Thessalonians 5:15		

Write Ephesians 6:1–3.

_____

_____

_____

_____

_____

_____

_____

Across the Centuries: Level E:
Anne of Green Gables
Copyright © 1998 Convention Press

Master 5.1

Anne of Green Gables

EARLY 1900'S DRESS

Across the Centuries: Level E:
Anne of Green Gables
Copyright © 1998 Convention Press

Master 6.1

Anne of Green Gables

LYING

When is lying okay? According to the Bible, NEVER! Use the following verses to explain what God says about lying.

Reference:	God's rule:
Proverbs 6:17	
Proverbs 12:22	
Romans 1:25	
Colossians 3:9	
Titus 1:2	
Hebrews 6:18	
1 John 2:21	
Acts 5:4	
Psalm 34:13	
Proverbs 19:5	
Proverbs 19:9	
John 8:44	
Exodus 20:16	

If God never approves of lying, why do you think the people in the following stories did not get punished?

Rahab and the Spies
Joshua 2:1–6 _____

_____

_____

Hebrew midwives
Exodus 1:15–21 _____

_____

_____

Across the Centuries: Level E:
Anne of Green Gables
Copyright © 1998 Convention Press

Master 7.1

Anne of Green Gables

Fantasy vs. Reality

Fantasy:

❶ _____
❷ _____
❸ _____
❹ _____
❺ _____

Reality:

❶ _____
❷ _____
❸ _____
❹ _____
❺ _____

Could be fantasy or reality:

❶ _____
❷ _____
❸ _____
❹ _____
❺ _____

Across the Centuries: Level E:
Anne of Green Gables
Copyright © 1998 Convention Press

Master 10.1

Anne of Green Gables

The Person I Want to Become

Anne of Green Gables

WATCH YOUR TONGUE

Look up the following verses:

Psalm 34:13	Psalm 37:30	Proverbs 10:19
Proverbs 17:20	James 3:8	Proverbs 26:28
Ephesians 4:15, 29–30	Colossians 4:6	

Apply what you learn from these verses to each of the following situations. For each scenario, write two or three sentences explaining how things should have been done differently.

❶ Julie and Sydney are good friends. Julie wanted to phone Sydney's ex-friend, so she asked Sydney if that would be okay. At first, Sydney seemed fine with the idea, but now she is spreading rumors about Julie flirting with boys. How should Julie respond?

❷ Jessica was upset at school one day. She shared her frustration about Amy with her best friend, Sarah. When Mark came and sat next to them, Jessica kept complaining about Amy. She trusted Mark to keep quiet. The next day, Amy confronted Jessica with all the things that she said. Jessica believes Mark spread the gossip. Now it's a huge mess.

❸ Patrick and Ryan are best friends and have always shared a friendly competition. However, when Patrick was chosen for first chair in band, Ryan said it was because his dad was rich and could buy the new uniforms the band needed. He never thought that his comments would be printed in the gossip column of the school newspaper.

❹ Chad and Monica have been friends since fifth grade. One day Chad was complaining to his friends about something that Monica did, and eventually Monica was told about it. She was hurt, so she said something negative in return. Now their friends are continually repeating the hurtful messages that keep going back and forth between the two.

❺ No one likes Mrs. Battle, and everyone talks about her outside of class. One student, who prides herself on her honesty, decided to have a talk with Mrs. Battle. Instead of helping the situation, Mrs. Battle was deeply offended and is now more strict and unfriendly than ever.

❻ TeriAnne heard that Andy's parents were getting a divorce. While responding to requests for prayer, she mentioned Andy's parents and elaborated with her own ideas as to their reasons. Her ideas have now been reported as true throughout the school.

Across the Centuries: Level E:
Anne of Green Gables
Copyright © 1998 Convention Press

Master 13.1

Anne of Green Gables

EMBARRASSING SCENARIOS

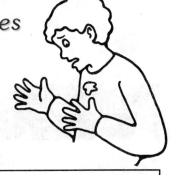

Act out the following scenarios; write your own endings.

❶ Kelly is the new girl at school. She just hasn't been able to fit in. Finally, they are going to play softball in P.E. This is a sport in which she excels. As she walks to the plate for her first at-bat, she is sure she will find her place in the school. By accident, the pitcher throws a crazy pitch. It hits Kelly in the stomach. She's not seriously hurt but is unable to bat. Everyone laughs at the pitcher's lack of control, but Kelly feels that they are laughing at her. What should she do?

❷ Jeff has wanted to make a good impression on Stacey. He finally gets the nerve to talk to her at lunch. As he walks toward her table, she looks up and blushes. He sees her friend lean over and whisper, and they both start to giggle. As he talks to her, he has a feeling that they are laughing at him, but he is glad that he finally introduced himself. Later, in the restroom he discovers that he has pizza stains all over the front of his shirt. That must have been what they were laughing about. What should he do?

❸ Andrea has been waiting for the spring concert all year. Her mom bought her a beautiful new dress since she has a solo to sing. When she arrives, she notices that another girl has the exact same dress, and this girl is singing right before Andrea. What should she do?

❹ It is Rachel's fourteenth birthday, and she made some cookies to take to school for her special day. As her classmates begin to eat them, they get funny looks on their faces and then spit them out. When asked what is wrong, they say that the cookies are extremely salty. Suddenly Rachel realizes that she must have put salt into the recipe instead of sugar. How is she going to live this down?

❺ Eric's parents do not want him to just hang out at the mall. After meeting some friends at the library, he joins them in going to the mall to play video games. The librarian finds Eric's books and calls his parents to report that they have been found. When Eric returns home, he is unprepared for his parents' questions. What should he do?

Across the Centuries: Level E:
Anne of Green Gables
Copyright © 1998 Convention Press

Anne of Green Gables

JOBS FOR THE FUTURE

Occupation	Education	Training	Skills
Accountant			
Nurse			
Doctor			
Electrician			
Teacher			
Farmer			
Pastor			
Mechanical Engineer			
Actor			
Attorney			
Author			
Interior Designer			
Travel Agent			
Missionary			
Psychologist			
Congressional Representative			

Across the Centuries: Level E:
Anne of Green Gables
Copyright © 1998 Convention Press

Master 15.1

Anne of Green Gables

ANNE: THEN AND NOW

For each of the areas listed, compare Anne in the beginning of the book with how she has grown up. Are any of the areas still the same?

	Appearance	
	Talkativeness	
	Getting into mischief	
	Temper	
	Diligence to studies	
	Manners	
	Impulsiveness	
	Relationships	
	Special friendships	
	Loyalty	

Anne of Green Gables

MATTHEW'S EPITAPH

If you were writing the tribute to Matthew on his tombstone, what would you say?

Matthew Cuthbert

 # Anne of Green Gables

UNIT TEST

I. Matching

____ ❶ Anne's chief rival   A. Anne Shirley
____ ❷ Avonlea's gossip and busybody   B. Marilla Cuthbert
____ ❸ a talkative orphan   C. Matthew Cuthbert
____ ❹ Anne's best friend   D. Diana Barry
____ ❺ shy around all women   E. Gilbert Blythe
____ ❻ wins the Avery scholarship   F. Mrs. Rachel Lynde
____ ❼ buys Anne a dress with puffed sleeves
____ ❽ believes that children should be raised with discipline
____ ❾ apologizes to Anne several times
____ ❿ loves Anne but cannot express her feelings well

II. True/False: If the answer is false, change the statement so that it is true.

_____ ❶ Aunt Josephine blames Anne for getting Diana drunk.

_____ ❷ Anne's parents died from the fever.

_____ ❸ Gilbert is Anne's biggest rival in school.

_____ ❹ Anne is not allowed to go to the concert because she supposedly lost Marilla's amethyst brooch.

_____ ❺ Miss Stacy is Anne's new Sunday school teacher.

_____ ❻ Marilla talks Anne into apologizing to Mrs. Rachel.

_____ ❼ Anne accepts a teaching job at the Carmody school.

_____ ❽ Marilla could have sent Anne to live with Mrs. Blewett.

_____ ❾ Anne's worst subject is English.

_____ ❿ Marilla is slowly going deaf.

Across the Centuries: Level E:
Anne of Green Gables
Copyright © 1998 Convention Press

III. Short Answer

1. Why did Anne go back to school after she was no longer allowed to see Diana?

2. Why did Anne know what to do for Minnie Mae's croup?

3. Why was Anne so adamant that she had to walk the ridgepole?

4. Why was Anne disappointed in the dresses Marilla made for her?

5. How did Anne mess up the cake when she was trying to impress Mrs. Allan?

6. What was unique about Miss Stacy's teaching style?

7. Why did Matthew feel that Anne needed a new dress with puffed sleeves?

8. What color was Anne trying to dye her hair when it turned green?

9. What did Gilbert say he would never do again after Anne rejected him for the second time?

10. Who told Anne that Gilbert had given her the Avonlea school?

11. What age was Anne when she went to Green Gables?

12. What was in the carpetbag Anne brought to Green Gables?

13. What was the name Anne wished she had been given?

IV. Essay Questions

1. How was Anne a good example of the following character traits: loyalty, honesty and acceptance?

2. Based on Biblical ideas concerning friendship, explain why Anne was a good friend to Diana Barry.

3. Explain three foreshadowing elements in this story.